Death is Just a Doorway

Amazing Accounts
of the Afterlife

(A revision of the previously published book,
Where Do We Go from Here?)

*Insights into the afterlife gleaned from teachings of the
leaders of the Church of Jesus Christ of Latter-day Saints*
and from gospel-confirming near-death experiences*

Wesley M. White
with
Richard E. McDermott

*This is not an official Church publication

Death is Just a Doorway

Copyright © 2024 by Wesley M. White

All rights reserved. No part of this book may be reproduced in any form without permission from the author, except as permitted by U.S. copyright law.

To request permission, contact Wesley M. White at wesnkay@gmail.com

Printed in the U.S.A.

ISBN 9798329755749

White Rose Books

Bible quotes are from the King James Version (KJM)
Original cover image is by fietzfotos from Pixabay

Praise for
Death is Just a Doorway

Death is Just a Doorway is fascinating and inspiring. Very well researched and a pleasure to read. Once I started, I had to keep reading, and I found myself thinking about it all through the day. I highly recommend it!"

— *Chris Stewart, NY Times best-sellling author, Former US congressman*

"One of the best books I have ever read. I wholeheartedly recommend it. It will complement and strengthen your faith and belief in the afterlife, as well as bringing you peace, happiness, and comfort as you anticipate our next life."

— *Warren Butler, MD*

"I've had questions about the afterlife since my little brother was killed in 2010. In fact, I've been certainly a little frustrated that I not only didn't know more, but couldn't find what I thought was credible, accurate, and detailed info about the spirit world. Wesley's book drew me in instantly."

— *Thaddeus, online book reviewer*

"After my dad's three-year battle with cancer came to an end, I found solace in Wes's book. It served as a beacon of hope. Soon thereafter, my mother departed suddenly. Once again, I turned to Wes's book, drawing even more insight. I reveled in the joyful possibilities of what my parents might be experiencing. I am immensely grateful for the solace and strength this book has provided in my most challenging times of life."

— *Reagan Price, mother of three*

"I loved this book! It made a lot of sense to me and was easy to read. I just purchased another for a friend."

— *Sharon Spencer, mother and philanthropist*

Wesley M. White

"This book is very well researched and fluidly written. I had a tough time putting it down! The research for this book was obviously extensive. To me, it is reassuring that all these sources tend to harmonize and support each other regarding the main characteristics of the afterlife."

— *Wayne Gelder, retired programmer*

"This book is outstanding. White clearly did what must have been thousands of hours of research on the afterlife, and compiled various accounts and experiences, as well as what great thinkers have to say on the matter and has laid it out in a compelling and comprehensive way."

— *Kevin Jensen, entrepreneur*

"I loved everything about this book! I think everyone should have a copy. It explains the Spirit World in an understandable way. I will be reading and studying it for years to come."

— *Rachel Johnson, cystic fibrosis survivor*

Table of Contents

Dedication... xi
A Quick Guide to the Individuals Quoted in this Book........ xiii
Introduction xvii
    The History of NDEs.. xix
    The Medical Community's Response........................ xx
    Sources... xx
    Definitions... xxi
        Premortality (Our life before our birth)................ xxi
        Mortality... xxii
    Primary Objectives xxiii
    Heavenly Father's Plan of Salvation...................... xxiv
Chapter 1 — Premorality: Our Life Before Our Birth........... 1
    NOTES 6
Chapter 2 — Rachel's and Kristy's Near-Death
                Experiences.. 9
    Rachel's Experience... 9
    Kristy's Experience... 14
    NOTE... 19
Chapter 3 — Through a Glass, Darkly........................... 21
    Spirit World Basics... 27
    NOTES 28
Chapter 4 — Was the Length of Our Life on Earth
                Set Before Our Birth?............................ 29
    NOTES 32
Chapter 5 — Does God Have a Particular Earthly
                Mission for Each of His Children?............. 33
    Character Built Through Crisis................................ 35

An Orderly Universe.. 36
Our Tailor-Made Trials.. 37
Rachel's Experience... 39
NOTES.. 39

Chapter 6 — The Most Common Near-Death Experiences... 41
Out of Body Experiences... 42
Life Reviews... 42
Passing Through a Tunnel... 43
Meeting a Loving Being of Light.. 44
Seeing Deceased Relatives... 45
NOTES.. 46

Chapter 7 — Progress in the Spirit World...........................47
NOTES.. 55

Chapter 8 — An Overview of Hell, and the Other
       Low Realms..57
Hell... 57
Other Low Realms... 60
"Ghosts"... 62
A Warning to Us.. 63
NOTES.. 63

Chapter 9 — An Overview of Paradise and the Other
       Higher Realms... 65
Paradise.. 65
The Higher Realms.. 68
The Amazing Visit... 69
NOTES.. 73

Chapter 10 — Where Is the Spirit World?........................... 75
Rachel's Experience... 78
NOTES.. 79

Chapter 11 — Do We Have Guardian/Ministering Angels?... 81
Our Personal Experience..84

Angels Ministering Within the Spirit World............... 84
Spirit World "Halls of Rest"................................. 86
Rachel's Experience.. 88
Summary... 88
NOTES... 89

Chapter 12 — Temples in the Spirit World..................... 91
Rachel's Experience.. 94
NOTES... 94

Chapter 13 — Missionary Work in the Spirit World 95
NOTES... 97

Chapter 14 — Time, Space, Expeditions, and Discoveries
    in the Spirit World...................................... 99
Rachel's Experience... 101
Space.. 102
Travel... 102
The Academia of the City.................................... 103
Animation.. 105
The Physical Brain and the Eternal Mind.................... 108
World History... 109
Technology.. 110
Research.. 111
NOTES... 112

Chapter 15 — Color and Music in the Spirit World.......... 115
Color... 115
Music... 115
The Special Relationship Between Music and Color.... 116
The Concert... 117
NOTES... 117

Chapter 16 — Sociality in the Spirit World.................. 119
Spirit World Occupations................................... 121
Spirit World Animals....................................... 123

- Birds.. 123
- Husbands and Wives... 124
- Families Are Forever..126
- NOTES.. 128

Chapter 17 — Learning in the Spirit World................... 129
- Thirst for Knowledge...129
- All Knowledge... 130
- Assisted Learning.. 131
- Continued Learning... 131
- Students...132
- Teachers...133
- Libraries...134
- Multimedia..135
- Some Final Points... 135
- Rachel's Experience... 135
- NOTES.. 136

Chapter 18 — The Spirits of Children............................139
- A Mother's Sacrifice.. 142
- A Child's NDE... 143
- Rachel's Experience... 145
- NOTES.. 145

Chapter 19 — How the Spirit Differs from the Body......... 147
- The Immortal Mind... 149
- Anatomy and Physiology of Our Spirits................... 153
- NOTES.. 155

Chapter 20 — Freedom from Frustration..................... 157

NOTES.. 160

Chapter 21 — How Does an NDE Affect the Rest of One's Mortal Life?.................................... 161
- Rachel's Experience... 163

NOTES	165
Chapter 22 — Transition to the Spirit World	167
The Other Side of the Veil	172
Rachel's Experience	175
NOTES	175
Chapter 23 — Divine Light and Love	177
A Testimony	180
NOTES	182
Chapter 24 — The Divine Role of Jesus Christ in Our Next Life	183
God the Father's Eternal Mission	184
Jesus Christ's Great Earthly Ministry	184
His Greater Message	185
His Greatest Gift	186
A Remarkable Testimony of Gethsemane	188
NOTES	191
Author Biography	193
Acknowledgements	194
WORKS CITED	195
INDEX	201

Wesley M. White

Dedication

For all of my adult life, I have been an avid bargain hunter: cars, motorcycles, books, clothes (but not boats—no boat has ever turned out to be a bargain). And when I consider something a bargain, it doubles my enjoyment.

I continued my bargain-hunting ways when seeking a wife. I dated Kay off and on for three and a half years, but even when we were "off," she was always in my heart. She still is. We have been married for 55 years, and each day I marvel and thrill at my treasured and priceless "bargain." I dedicate this book to her—may our mutual "copyright" never expire.

Wesley M. White

A Quick Guide to the Individuals Quoted in this Book

Alexander, Eben — Author of *Proof of Heaven* (2012).

Amrine, Kristy Shaw — Niece of the author's wife, Kay.

Andersen, Rachel Potter — Daughter of a close friend and neighbor of the author.

Arrington, Leonard J. — Author of *Brigham Young, American Moses* (2012).

Benson, Ezra Taft — Former President of the Church of Jesus Christ of Latter-day Saints who served as the Prophet from 1985–1994.

Benson, Robert Hugh — The books by Anthony Borgia (listed in the entry just below) were dictated to him by Benson.

Borgia, Anthony — Author of *Heaven and Earth* (1995); *Here and Hereafter* (1968); *Life in the World Unseen* (1993); and *More About Life in the World Unseen* (2000).

Burpo, Todd — Author (with Vincent, Lynn) of *Heaven Is for Real* (2010).

Callister, Tad R. — Author of *The Infinite Atonement* (2000).

Clark, J. Reuben — First Counselor to President David O. McKay, 1959–1961.

Crowther, Duane S. — Author of *Life Everlasting: A Definitive Study of Life After Death* (1967).

Faust, James E. — A member of the Quorum of the Twelve Apostles of the Church of Jesus Christ of Latter-day Saints. Served as the Second Counselor in the First Presidency, 1995–2007.

Eadie, Betty J. — Author of *Embraced by the Light* (1992).

Gong, Gerritt W. — A member of the Quorum of the Twelve Apostles. Ordained in 2018.

Grant, Heber J. — Former President of the Church of Jesus Christ of Latter-day Saints who served as the Prophet from 1918–1945.

Haraldsson, Erlendur, PhD (and Osis, Karlis, PhD). — Author of *At the Hour of Death* (1997).

Harnsberger, Caroline Thomas — Author of *Mark Twain at Your Fingertips, A Book of Quotations*, Dover Publications, 2009

Hill, Mary V. — Author of *Angel Children* (1973).

Hinckley, Gordon B. — Former President of the Church of Jesus Christ of Latter-day Saints who served as the Prophet from 1995–2008.

Holland, Jeffrey R. — Acting President of the Quorum of the Twelve Apostles. Ordained in 1994.

Hunter, Howard W. — Former President of the Church of Jesus Christ of Latter-day Saints who served as the Prophet from 1994–1995.

Ingersoll, Robert Green — An American lawyer and writer, nicknamed "the Great Agnostic" (1833–1899).

Jensen, Ellen — A member of the Church of Jesus Christ of Latter-day Saints.

Johnson, Benjamin — A member of the Church of Jesus Christ of Latter-day Saints.

Kimball, Heber C. — First Counselor to Brigham Young, serving 1847–1868.

Kimball, Spencer W. — Former President of the Church of Jesus Christ of Latter-day Saints who served as the Prophet from 1973–1985.

Klebingat, Jorg — A General Authority Seventy of the Church. Sustained in 2014.

Lee, Harold B. — Former President of the Church of Jesus Christ of Latter-day Saints who served as the Prophet from 1972–1973.

Lehi — An ancient prophet in The Book of Mormon.

Lewis, C. S. — Author of *Mere Christianity* (1943) and many other books.

Lundahl, Craig — Author of the article "Angels in Near-Death Experiences," in the Journal of Near-Death Studies (1992).

Vickie M. — "Out of Body Experience." NDE, NDERF, www.nderf.org/nderfexplorer/nderf_.html, retrieved January 10, 2022.

MacDonald, George — A Scottish writer of several works of Christian theology and a mentor of C. S. Lewis.

Maxwell, Neal A. — A member of the Quorum of the Twelve Apostles, serving 1981–2004.

McConkie, Bruce R. — A member of the Quorum of the Twelve Apostles, serving 1972–1985.

Menet, Sarah LaNell — Author of *There Is No Death* (2002).

Moody, Raymond — Author of *Life after Life* (1975), *The Light Beyond* (1988), and *Reflections on Life After Life* (1978).

Neal, Mary C. — Author of *To Heaven and Back* (2013).

Nelson, Lee — Author of *Beyond the Veil* (1988).

Osis, Karlis and Haraldsson, Erlundur — Authors of *At the Hour of Death* (1997).

Packer, Boyd K. — Former President of the Quorum of the Twelve Apostles, serving 2008–2015.

Pratt, Orson — An original member of the Quorum of the Twelve Apostles, called in 1835.

Pratt, Parley P. — An original member member of the Quorum of the Twelve Apostles, serving 1835–1857.

Rampton, Ryan J. — Author of *You Were Born a Warrior: A Near Death Experience* (2018).

Ring, Kenneth, PhD — Author of *Heading Toward Omega* (1984).

Ritchie, George G., Jr. — Author of *Ordered to Return* (1998) and *Return from Tomorrow* (1978) with Elizabeth Sherrill.

Rotstein, Gary — Author of the article "Near Death, Seeing Dead People May Be Neither Rare nor Eerie." *Standard Examiner* Newspaper, Ogden, UT: July 10, 2018.

Samuel the Lamanite — A Book of Mormon prophet.

Scott, Richard G. — A member of the Quorum of the Twelve Apostles, serving 1988–2015.

Si, William — "Meeting a Loving Being of Light." NDERF, www.nderf.org/nderfexplorer/nderf_.html, retrieved January 10, 2002

Smith, Lucy Mack — Mother of the Prophet Joseph Smith and author of *The Revised and Enhanced History of Joseph Smith by His Mother* (1996).

Smith, Joseph, Jr. — Founder and first President of the Church of Jesus Christ of Latter-day Saints. He saw God the Father and His Son Jesus Christ in a vision at the age of 14 and subsequently translated the Book of Mormon.

Smith, Joseph F. — A Former President of the Church of Jesus Christ of Latter-day Saints and nephew of the Prophet Joseph Smith.

Sobes, Victor Z. — "Going Through a Tunnel." NDERF, www.nderf.org/nderfexplorer/nderf.html, retrieved January 10, 2022.

Springer, Rebecca Ruter — Author of *My Dream of Heaven* (2009).

Swedenborg, Emanuel — A visionary (1688–1772) who is quoted in Brent and Wendy Top's book *Glimpses Beyond Death's Door*.

Top, Brent L. and Wendy C. — Authors of *Glimpses Beyond Death's Door* (2012).

Yancey, Philip — Author of *The Jesus I Never Knew* (1995).

Young, Brigham — Former President of the Church of Jesus Christ of Latter-day Saints who served as the Prophet from 1847–1877.

Introduction

My interest in the spirit world began in 1987. It was a rare, beautiful February day as my wife, Kay, drove along in our old pickup, windows down, a hint of spring in the air.

This was long before child safety seats were required, and our seventh child, two-and-a-half-year-old Russell, was next to her, his little arm around her shoulders. As she drove, Kay experienced an unanticipated communication from the Holy Spirit.

It came in the form of a simple, clear question: *You have had life quite smooth for a while; are you ready for a trial?* Her mind recoiled with a strident *No!* but her spirit recognized the moment as a time of necessary compliance, and she softly whispered, *Yes.*

We were living the dream. We fell in love with Utah, and I loved my US Air Force assignment, flying an interesting and fulfilling mission. Primary Children's Hospital was a wonderful resource for our mentally handicapped fourth child, Debbie. Life was good.

How quickly Life can take a different turn!

That "turn" came within days of Kay's spiritual communication. My aircraft crew was in the office, preparing for a flight, when a crew member announced, "Wes, there's a call for you from your next-door neighbor." Because our office phone number was unlisted, that seemed highly unusual. I knew that it had to be something important, whether good or bad. I took the call, and the neighbor blurted, "Russell has been hit by a car!" When I asked if Russell was seriously injured, she hung up.

The drive home was the longest twenty minutes of my life. *Did Russell have a broken arm—perhaps a serious head injury? Could it be that he...?* I couldn't bear to let the thought even enter my mind.

I arrived home to the scene of so many ambulances, police cars, and emergency vehicles that I had to park more than a block away. As I sprinted home, a paramedic almost tackled me. He said, "Your little boy did not survive the impact. Do you want to spend a moment with him?"

He pointed to an ambulance. Little Russell's body was still warm, though disfigured. As I embraced my son for the last time, an ecclesiastical leader approached me and said, "Wes, you are needed in the house. Kay is blaming herself."

Recognizing that severe trials are a part of almost every life, I won't "grieve" you (*Daniel 7:15*) with the details of our walk through "the valley of the shadow of death" (*Psalm 23:4*). It is probably familiar territory to you.

Kay and I had lost parents, but this was different. Russell was a little child. He had completely depended on us for all his needs.

Others tried to comfort us by saying, "Russell was called on a mission to the spirit world." You'll understand our reaction: *Yes, but he never writes.* We didn't doubt that he lived on, but we very much wanted to know more about his "world." *Was he being cared for now? Did he miss us? Was his spirit an adult or a child? Will he ever have a "helpmeet?"* (*Genesis 2:18*)

We concurred with Robert Ingersoll's lamentation on page 179 of the book *Greatest Speeches of Col. R. G. Ingersoll:* "The poor barbarian, weeping above his dead, can answer these questions just as well as the robed priest of the most authentic creed."

These and so many unanswered questions inspired me with a

deeply personal motive to research our next life. I felt compelled to publish my findings to share with others who had lost a loved one and who also desire more answers.

The History of NDEs

The human family has probably experienced "near-death experiences" (referred to as NDEs) for thousands of years. Most did not communicate these experiences beyond a few people due to the risk of persecution. During the Middle Ages and even the Renaissance, if someone experienced and then spoke of an NDE, he or she was likely regarded as a witch and burned at the stake. Even into the mid-twentieth century, the subject of what began being called the near-death experience was rarely discussed in public venues. Those who told such stories were shut down by physicians, relatives, and friends who believed that such talk was the result of anesthesia, post-surgery hallucinations, or even mental illness.

The eruption of shared NDE experiences didn't really begin until the 1970s, when George G. Ritchie, Jr.'s story was published. He had technically "died" while a soldier during World War II. Hospital records verified that he had died for nine minutes and was then resuscitated. He knew that he had died and that he had indeed had an incredible experience that would have required several weeks to transpire. He had shared his experience sparingly because it usually engendered negative responses, if not hostility. He continued his scientific education, earning an M.D. and then completing a residency in psychiatry. He determined that his NDE was too real and too complex to be a figment of his imagination. He considered it a testament that should be widely revealed. Therefore, in 1978, Ritchie wrote a book detailing his NDE, titled *Return from Tomorrow*. The book is still selling millions of copies.

My own copy is from its 29th printing. Ritchie includes his account of meeting the Savior and feeling of His character and love, learning that He knows all of us individually, and that His love for us is the strongest force in the universe. (To better understand Christ's role after this life, refer to the Appendix: The Divine Role of Jesus Christ in the Next Life.)

Ritchie's story inspired Dr. Raymond Moody to begin scientific research on NDEs. His first book, *Life After Life*, sold over 13 million copies, and he has written three additional books on the subject. Since Ritchie's and Moody's work, the NDE market has exploded.

The Medical Community's Response

Even when medical advances allowed physicians to resuscitate patients who were clinically dead, NDEs were shrugged off as unexplored phenomena of a malfunctioning human brain. Generally, the initial reaction by the medical community was skepticism. However, as eminent and trusted patients shared experiences, and as NDEs reported by patients correlated with facts (such as the blind lady who described her surgery and the associated surgical instruments), it became clear that many NDEs were indeed validated by the physical world.

Perhaps out of curiosity, other physicians began questioning their patients and were surprised at the number of stories that came to light, stories that confirmed Moody's findings. Since then, dozens of studies by credentialed researchers have corroborated Moody's work.

Sources

The increased research and acceptance of NDEs have resulted in greater public interest, which has in turn produced an explosion of books, documentaries, and programs on the subject. Some are certainly valid, but there is suspicion that many reports have been dramatically enhanced or even falsified.

I have diligently strived with every word to be in harmony with the Gospel of Jesus Christ. To help you feel the veracity of this book, here is the priority of sources utilized:

- General Authorities, particularly prophets and apostles: their experiences and official pronouncements.
- Physicians and scientists with verifiable credentials who have conducted scientific studies of near-death experiences.
- Members of The Church of Jesus Christ of Latter-day Saints who are scholarly yet humble, and individuals known personally by the author whose accounts are in harmony with Church doctrine.
- Others (Church members, and many who are not) who report near-death experiences that are in accord with others' experiences and with Church doctrine.
- Two or more credible witnesses whose experiences parallel each other.

Naturally, some sources have yielded far more information than have others. Therefore, the number of paragraphs from a particular source does not necessarily indicate its priority as a source.

Definitions

There are two essential terms that may be unfamiliar, but which are necessary for your understanding of the rest of this book:

Premortality (Our life before our birth)
The Church of Jesus Christ of Latter-day Saints is unique (as far as I know) among Christian faiths in its belief in a premortal

existence. Through the scriptures and proclamations of Latter-day prophets, we know that prior to coming to this mortal world, we dwelt with a Heavenly Father and a Heavenly Mother. This must have been a beautiful existence, one where we were taught those things that would make us more like our Heavenly Parents—things that ultimately would help us to receive a fullness of joy. Chapter 1, "Premortality: Our Life Before Our Birth," provides much more information concerning this abode.

Mortality

This earth life. Suffice it to say that there came a point in our premortality when we had learned as much as we could in that stage of existence. To continue in our development, it would be necessary to come to earth, receive a body, and work through the challenges and vicissitudes of life—to learn good from evil. We could no longer, figurately, touch the stove and not get our fingers burned. It's a tough program with a wide variety of experiences eliciting joy, pain, exultation, misery, hope, and hopelessness, including a body that provides many opportunities but denies us many others. We are here to be tried (and isn't that trial often severe?) and to gain experience (and aren't some of those experiences something we wish could be avoided?).

Now, for the meat of this work—a greatly abridged account of our next life (excluding the final judgment and the ultimate kingdoms of glory, the which are beyond the scope of this study). May it, by providing you a wider understanding, enhance your life and give meaning to your challenges—which are by no means random.

Primary Objectives

- This book's first intent is to comfort those who have lost loved ones. You will discover that most who have passed are in an environment more desirable than they ever dreamed possible, where, because of the Atonement, they continue to progress!

- The second intent is to ameliorate the debilitating fear of dying. It is natural to fear the unknown. Yet there is so much more that is known about the next life that goes unshared. There is not a spirit world Wikipedia. However, this study is as close as you will find. And as you study and search, you will discover that, for the most part, the next life is a land of enhancements.

- The third intent is to inspire you to make those tweaks to your mortal life that will help you be even more prepared to meet God.

Wesley M. White

Heavenly Father's
Plan of Salvation
Implemented by Our Savior, Jesus Christ

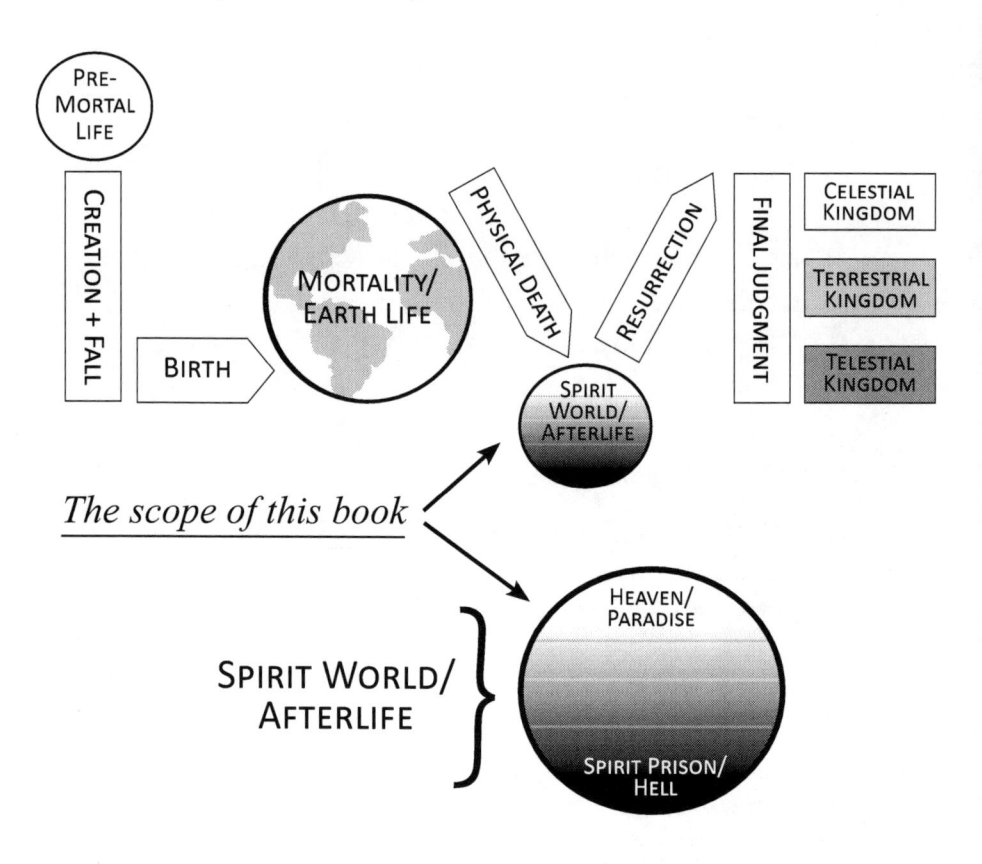

- Pre-Mortal Life
- Creation + Fall
- Birth
- Mortality/Earth Life
- Physical Death
- Spirit World/Afterlife
- Resurrection
- Final Judgment
- Celestial Kingdom
- Terrestrial Kingdom
- Telestial Kingdom

The scope of this book

Spirit World/Afterlife
- Heaven/Paradise
- Spirit Prison/Hell

Chapter 1
Premortality: Our Life Before Our Birth

> "Before I formed thee in the belly, I knew thee; and before thou camest forth out of the womb I sanctified thee, and I ordained thee a prophet unto the nations."
> — *Jeremiah 1:5*

Preparing for Judgment Day is like being in a three-act play. Before we entered mortality, we lived with God as His spirit children—the first act of our "play." While our existence was undoubtedly pleasant, it was inadequate to prepare us for what we had the potential to become. We had to learn more through the experience of a mortal life, where we would be tried and strengthened through difficulties, disappointments, and events that would test our faith. We had to learn firsthand the difference between good and evil.

Our physical birth began the second act, and it certainly lives up to its billing, giving us a broad range of experiences from exhilarating to devastating.

The third act begins upon death, when we transition to the next world. Here we will continue to learn and progress as we prepare for Judgment Day.

Said Elder Neal A. Maxwell (one of the Twelve Apostles of

the Church of Jesus Christ of Latter-day Saints—hereinafter "the Church"): "If we could see man in continuum (all three 'acts') then we could both understand and rejoice more in the plan of life."[1]

While the rest of this book is dedicated to act three, we will now discuss several elements of our premortal experience essential to our better understanding of the next world, and the joy we should feel in this life.

First, we who believe in a premortal existence are a minority. Many Christian denominations believe that only Jesus Christ existed premortally, inconsistent with God's declaration to Jeremiah: "Before I formed thee in the belly, I knew thee; and before thou camest forth out of the womb I sanctified thee, and I ordained thee a prophet unto the nations" (*Jeremiah 1:5*)

Elder Maxwell relates that in Judaism, both the Talmud (the primary source of Jewish religious law) and the Midrash (a textual interpretation of the Talmud) "clearly teach the doctrine of the premortal existence of souls."[2]

How and why did Christianity lose such an important doctrine? Dr. George Ritchie, author of *Ordered to Return* and *Return from Tomorrow*, submits that the Fifth Ecumenical Council of 533 AD rejected the belief in a premortal existence.[3] Elder Maxwell suggests this was done in an attempt to reduce personal accountability for our actions in this life.[4]

Second, our time spent in mortality is much shorter than that spent in our other two stages of existence, or "estates."

Again, to quote Elder Maxwell: "Compared to the first and third estates, the second estate is a mere afternoon."[5]

Third, in the first act (premortal life) we possessed agency (freedom of choice), reasoning powers, and intelligence. However, performance there varied greatly.

Elder Jörg Klebingat of the Quorum of the Seventy taught:

Opportunities for growth and learning were widely available. However, equal access to the teachings of a loving heavenly home did not produce a uniform desire among us—Heavenly Father's spirit children—to listen, learn, and obey. Exercising our agency, as we do today, we listened with varying degrees of interest and intent.

Some of us eagerly sought to learn and obey. With the war in heaven on the horizon, we prepared for graduation from our premortal home. Truth was taught and challenged; testimonies were borne and ridiculed, with each premortal spirit making the choice to either defend or defect from the Father's plan.[6]

Fourth, our performance in that first estate, as well as the characteristics of godhood that we still lack as we transition to mortality, greatly influence our mortal circumstances and assignments. Said Elder Maxwell:

Individuals have a genetic and an environmental inheritance, each of which is powerfully important. But there is an even earlier bestowal that follows us from our pre-mortal existence wherein our personalities and traits were developed in various ways and in various degrees and strengths. All three combined would, if fully comprehended, give us a true picture of the human personality and how it has been shaped and molded.[7]

Elder Maxwell expounds:

If one's responsibilities [in mortality] are in some ways linked to past performance or to past capabilities, it should not surprise us. When we say God has a plan, he truly has a plan—not simply a grand scale, but for each of us as individuals, allocating some special talent to this dispensation and some to another.

I regard God as the perfect personnel manager, even though he must work with and through all of us who are so imperfect.

I assume, gladly, that in the allocation to America of remarkable leaders like Thomas Jefferson, George Washington, and Abraham Lincoln, the Lord was just as careful. After all, if you've got only one Abraham Lincoln, you'd better put him in that point in history when he's most needed—much as some of us might like to have him now. There cannot be a plan for the whole without a plan for each part. God knew beforehand each of our coefficients for coping and contributing.[8]

He subsequently states:

> When in situations of stress we wonder if there is any more in us to give, we can be comforted to know that God, who knows our capacity perfectly, placed us here to succeed. No one was foreordained to fail or to be wicked. When we feel overwhelmed, let us recall the assurance given through Joseph [Smith] that God, who knows we 'cannot bear all things now,' [D&C 78:18] will not over program us; he will not press upon us more than we can bear.[9]

No doubt, there are individuals given special challenges like he who was "blind from birth" (*John 9: 1-2.*) Some come to bring glory to God. Maxwell warns us:

> We must, however, be exceedingly careful about imputing either wrong causes or wrong rewards to any of such. They are in the Lord's hands, and he loves them perfectly. Some of those who have required much waiting upon in this life may be waited upon in the next world—but for the highest of reasons.[10]

It is reasonable to assume, therefore, that a person who was valiant in the premortal life could be born into abject poverty because his covenant mortal assignment required him to live among the poorest of the poor.

Fifth, our premortal preparation included both a "general education" provided to all mortals, as well as specialized training for our particular mortal mission.

Elder Maxwell taught: "There cannot be a grand plan of salvation for all mankind, unless there is also a plan for each individual.

The salvational sum will reflect all its parts."[11]

Sixth, our first and second estates feature very different learning environments.

Said Elder Maxwell:

> Our first estate featured learning of a cognitive type, and it was surely a much longer span than that of our second estate, and the tutoring so much better and more direct. The second estate, however, is one that emphasizes experiential learning through applying, proving, and testing. We learn cognitively here too, just as a good university examination also teaches even as it tests us.
>
> In any event, the books of the first estate are now closed to us, and the present test is, therefore, very real. We have moved, as it were, from first-estate theory to second-estate laboratory. It is here that our Christ-like characteristics are further shaped, and our spiritual skills are thus strengthened.
>
> Such a transition in emphasis understandably produces genuine anxiety, for to be 'proved herewith' suggests a stern test, a test that must roll forward to completion or else all that has been invested up to that point would be at risk.[12]

Seventh, as mentioned earlier, our first three estates constitute a continuum.

Elder Bruce R. McConkie, a former apostle of the Church, taught: "All of us are separated by a thin veil only from the friends and fellow laborers with whom we served on the Lord's errand before our eternal spirits took up their abodes in tabernacles of clay."[13]

Finally, we came joyously to earth.

A previous President of the Church, Ezra Taft Benson, taught:

> We could hardly wait to demonstrate to our Father and our brother, the Lord, how much we loved them and how we would be obedient to Him, in spite of the earthly opposition of the evil one.

> Nothing is going to startle us more when we pass through the veil to the other side than to realize how well we know Our Father and how familiar His face is to us ... If we only knew it, there are heavenly hosts pulling for us—friends in heaven that we can't remember now, who yearn for our victory.[14]

In the next chapter, we will study the first of a myriad of near-death experiences (hereafter referred to as NDEs). Rachel Andersen recounts her personal NDE—which could also be referred to as her visit to the "third estate."

NOTES

1. Maxwell, Neal A., *The Promise of Discipleship*, 109. Elder Maxwell wrote more than thirty books. This particular book includes a chapter on the spirit world and was written just three years before his death following a six-year battle with cancer.

2. Maxwell, *But for a Small Moment*, 109. In Maxwell's typical, elegant prose, he compares the emphasis of the Prophet Joseph Smith's teaching before his incarceration in Liberty Jail with what he emphasized in his remaining years. Elder Maxwell postulates that the challenges of being the Prophet of the Restoration had kept him so occupied that he had little time to deeply study his revelations until he was confined for five months. Two chapters of his book are dedicated to the Prophet's post-imprisonment teachings about premortality.

3. Ritchie, George G., *Return from Tomorrow*, 141. Two of Dr. Ritchie's books, *Return from Tomorrow* and *Ordered to Return*, contribute substantially to this book. He is the great pioneer of NDE acceptance. He experienced a remarkable NDE in 1943, and after much encouragement from associates, published his first book. In his second book, *Ordered to Return*, he laments, "We all need to be ashamed of how we treated our Mormon brothers and sisters when they began" (p. 140). Dr. Ritchie inspired Dr. Raymond Moody in his extensive research of NDEs. Moody has interviewed thousands who have experienced this phenomenon. He has scientifically evaluated and categorized this information, publishing at least three books on the subject. On page 196 of his book, *Life After Death*, he states, "The Church of Jesus Christ of Latter-day Saints (the Mormons) have been aware of accounts of

near-death experiences for many years and circulate these stories among themselves."
4. Maxwell, 80.
5. Ibid.
6. Klebingat, Jörg, "Defending the Faith," *Ensign* Magazine, September 2009.
7. Maxwell, 99.
8. Maxwell, 89-90.
9. Ibid., 99.
10. Ibid., 102.
11. Ibid., 90.
12. Ibid.
13. McConkie, Bruce R., "God Ordained his Prophets and People," General Conference, April 1974.
14. Benson, Ezra T., "Jesus Christ—Gifts and Expectations," BYU Devotional address, December 1974.

Wesley M. White

Chapter 2
Rachel's and Kristy's Near-Death Experiences

> "I have experienced subsequent trials since my NDE, such as cancer, that have threatened my mortal life. Yet, through the power of the Holy Ghost, my spirit can commune with Father in Heaven, and I have realized again and again that He is truly over all things."
> — Rachel Andersen

I know several people who have experienced an NDE, and two of them I know very well. Both have been kind enough to write a synopsis of their experience for inclusion in this book. Their stories will enlighten and delight you.

Rachel's Experience

Rachel Potter Andersen is the daughter of one of my best friends, who has also been my next-door neighbor for nearly three decades. Through this prolonged and close relationship with my dear friend and neighbor, I naturally became well acquainted with his daughter Rachel's personality and high moral character.

Having full confidence that it is not in her nature to stretch or hyperbolize, I invited her to put her NDE in writing so that I could include it within this study. She has graciously agreed and here provides a firsthand account of an NDE—the kind of experience I have not had myself:

I was significantly blessed during my senior year in high school with a trial so great that it became necessary for me to completely rely on the Lord spiritually, physically, and mentally. This trial permanently altered my view of the temporal state of mortal life. Up to this time, I took my physical talents, mind, and abilities for granted and thought I had obtained achievements because of my own work and my own personal determination. Further, I believed I could accomplish any responsibility, challenge, or trial through my well-honed skills.

They were the center of my world—indeed, the biggest influence in my life.

My self-worth and testimony of the Savior had grown day by day, here a little and there a little, with each interaction and obedience to their advice.

Though not to the same degree, my friends, both at church and school, were also instrumental in my development. I was blessed to be surrounded with good, wholesome peers. I was involved in church and school leadership roles and took each task seriously. I excelled in academics and participated in student government, seminary council, extracurricular clubs, and piano lessons.

I served in my church class presidency, young women sports, and weekly activities. In short, I had a lot going on. I always did my best at all my assignments and aspired to be a good person. I demanded perfection of myself in fulfilling these obligations and was disappointed when I fell short. I honestly believed if I just tried hard enough, worked diligently enough, behaved well enough, and believed in myself, I could steer clear of any future trials or tribulations that would otherwise come.

Naively, I thought of my time on earth as everlasting. I fully identified with the hymn 'Because I Have Been Given Much' and acknowledged my responsibility that 'I too must give.' Although a developing trust in Christ and an increasing testimony of the spirit world were mine, a full reliance and trust in Jesus Christ were yet to be realized.

It was, quite literally, in a split second that my ideal lifestyle was shattered. All my hopes, dreams, and plans for my future seemed to be taken. A drunk driver came out of the dense fog that cold, fateful night, ran a red light, and hit my car broadside. I suffered multiple internal injuries and severe head trauma.

After several hours in surgery to repair my inner organs, I lay in a deep coma, eyes fixed and dilated, no reaction to pain, and unable to breathe or sustain regular body temperature. My Glasgow coma score was a three, only one point above brain dead. My parents were given no hope of my survival through the next twenty-four hours.

My father describes his pain during this time as 'bone deep and unrelenting.' Yet, our Father in Heaven promised that I would not only live but would also have a complete and total recovery. Such a promise was consequent to my past obedience to the commandments and will of the Lord.

After ten long days, I opened my eyes. Upon 'awakening,' amnesia and a long physical recovery followed. It seemed as if all was lost, but over time this has proven otherwise. The mortal miracle was clearly evident, and yet the bigger miracle could not be documented by simple medical facts and data.

No one knew what my spirit had experienced. As my physical body lay perfectly still, my spiritual self was elsewhere. The veil that typically separated the mortal and immortal worlds became unusually thin and the spirit world remarkably near. As a result, I personally saw and felt life after mortality. I was significantly blessed to spend time in the spirit world and, furthermore, to recall my sacred visit there.

A soft, delicate white mist of 'clean fog' permeated the room-like area, where I found myself. Relief washed over me as I saw before me my paternal grandmother, affectionately known to me as Gram. Although she had died of ovarian cancer six months before, here we stood face-to-face. Earnest love and tenderness enveloped me. I immediately remembered the eternal friendship we shared with one another. Gram held my gaze, her eyes emitting incredible energy and hope. Never had I known her hair to shine so brightly, her skin to be so smooth and milky white, or her lips and cheeks to be utterly flawless.

While Gram's physical beauty was truly exquisite, it was her extraordinary spiritual beauty that was most captivating. Her goodness and purity radiated a warm light that drew me to her closer. Our visit was intimately private and personal, and emphasized the importance of our time together. The exceptional trust ensured complete understanding. Despite our tenderness, Gram was composed, full of competence, intelligence, and wisdom.

Although I was aware of my current dire circumstances, I felt a sure sense of calmness and complete certainty regarding my future. I understood that my decision to continue my temporary earthly existence would affect my eternal existence. That assurance was so profound that all sense of worry or concern was completely alleviated.

Somehow Gram completely understood my thoughts before I could speak. I felt or sensed each answer to my questions. I knew of Gram's gentle encouragement to continue my earthly life. I was silently reminded of promises and blessings not yet fulfilled—most significantly that of motherhood. I realized I could only learn this level of joy and love through experiencing mortality, thereby easily recognizing the extreme importance of life yet to be made possible only through me. I felt no rush in my decision, yet there was no hesitation.

An all-encompassing sureness spread throughout my spirit, and immediately I realized my mortal mission was not yet complete. I knew I must resume my life on earth. I was filled with excitement and a strong sense of purpose. I felt no confusion or fear in my decision. It was as though I had made this choice before, possibly prior to my earthly existence, yet it was necessary to comply once again.

My time in the spirit world was not limited to my personal visit with Gram. I also communicated with my future children, maternal grandfather, and, most important, with the Godhead. I felt of Their presence near and sensed, had I desired, or had it been necessary, I could have visually seen Them, but I somehow knew and accepted that such was not needed. I knew of Father's full attention and support, as if we had spoken face-to-face. Communication and full comprehension were accomplished through the Holy Ghost. It was as though Father's thoughts were my own. As with Gram, sacred facts and guidance were transferred without voice, resulting in a detailed yet simple, pure perception of God's will. I was determined to be obedient and yet felt assured of His will that I must use my own agency. Such equanimity provided a sense of freedom as the Spirit of Truth testified to my spirit the correctness of my decision.

I returned to school a mere eight weeks following my NDE. I had missed an entire term and was overwhelmed by the amount of work it would take, just to be where I was before the accident. A wise and compassionate school counselor determined that 'my past was my future,' meaning that my previous hard work and good decisions would not go unnoticed.

I graduated with high honors, as I had planned. I continued with both speech and occupational therapy through that summer and then moved to Rexburg to pursue my education at Ricks College (now BYU-Idaho) on academic and leadership scholarships. Within two years, I graduated with my Associate's Degree in Interpersonal Communications. I then transferred to Utah State University, where I earned a bachelor's degree, cum laude, in family and human development.

I have been married for twenty-six years to a wonderful man, who gained a personal knowledge of Jesus Christ through much fasting and prayer during my recovery. Upon my return to my earthly existence, our relationship seemed natural, as if we had been good friends our entire lives. We experienced the Spirit testifying of truth together.

As I healed physically—taking my first steps, regaining my memory, relearning to drive, and so on—our connection, not only to one another but also to Christ, grew. He served for a time as a missionary for Christ in Japan following high school, and upon his return, we married a short six weeks later. We have four daughters and one son.

I have experienced subsequent trials since my NDE, such as cancer, that have threatened my mortal life. Yet, through the power of the Holy Ghost, my spirit can commune with Father in Heaven, and I have realized again and again that He is truly over all things. I know life spent in mortality is according to His will. As I plead for aid from those living on the other side of the veil, I am aware of their love. I realize pain and sorrow experienced on earth is temporary, but my testimony of the Lord's plan is eternal. A firm belief and absolute trust in an all-knowing eternal Father, as I have experienced in the spirit world, have been necessary to sustain me through such troubling times of uncertainty.

(Rachel's perspectives gained from her NDE are added to many chapters of this book).

Kristy's Experience

Kristy Shaw Amrine is our niece on my wife Kay's side. We know her a little better than we know Rachel because she is family. She possesses the same qualities and character as Rachel does.

When I was in second grade, a new boy in my class leaned across the aisle between our desks and said, 'Psst,' to get my attention. I had heard people say, 'Psst' on TV, I'd even read the word 'Psst' in books, but I had never heard anyone actually say it. He had my attention.

'Have you ever held a lizard?' he asked. The word lizard spoke to the tomboy in me. Soon we were talking every day about snakes and frogs and all things creepy and slimy. A lasting friendship had been cemented. We never had a problem from that day with finding something to talk about.

Through the years in our rural elementary school, we were in the same class until 6th grade. I soon outgrew my fascination with reptiles, but Travis and I found other things we had in common. We remained close, and our childhood friendship had established a special bond.

Travis and I both played the clarinet in Jr. High. It was totally a coincidence. We hadn't talked about it before we both joined band but here we were, together again, in band every day. There was a lot of sit-around-and-wait time in that class as the music teacher worked with each section. One of these times, the boys began to publicly rate the girls in the class.

When I later rebuked Travis for his behavior, he said I was a 'ten.' As I tried to hide the delight that was bubbling up inside me, he continued, "You have a pretty face, you're funny and nice, and you're not too fat and you're not too skinny and you have a cute butt." I squealed and swatted him, meaning to sound mortified, but I have to admit I was flattered. Travis was that way, always trying to build me up.

In high school, mutual friends brought us together again. We were in the same 'group.' Of course, we both soon had a crush on someone in the group. As Travis and I lamented our inability to attract our "crushes," he suggested we work as a team. "I'll call you tomorrow, and we will come up with a plan. I think we can help each other."

So that's how they began, daily phone calls that lasted for up to two hours. We spent a lot of time scheming, planning, and sharing our innermost feelings. Travis and I could talk about almost anything. I learned that Travis' confident exterior was hiding a lot of insecurities. I had always known that Travis was adopted as a baby, but I had never considered it an issue. I always thought adoption was nice. "It seems like there is nothing I can do to make my dad love me. Nothing I do is ever enough," he lamented.

I knew Travis's parents well enough to know that they loved him unconditionally, just like my parents did me, but for some reason he couldn't get it out of his head that he had to earn his father's love, and that his dad didn't stop loving him just because he messed up, and Travis messed up a lot.

One night when I came home from a date feeling aggravated and unappreciated, there was a message that Travis had called. That was the answer to my problems! He would be my savior! He would know what I should do. It was too late to call him that night, but I knew just where to find him before school in the morning. There was a bench in the hall where we, the game-and-movie-night group, always congregated, without fail, before the bell rang. Travis would be there. He would listen to my problem. He would know what to do.

The next morning, I arrived early at school. Only one member of our group was at the bench. 'Hey Casey, why do you look so down.'

'You haven't heard. Travis Hopkins shot himself last night.' Every bone in my body turned to mush.

'He got in a fight with his dad. He called Weston and asked if he wanted to go into the woods behind his house and shoot birds. Travis didn't wait for Weston, so Weston went out to look for him. He found him with a gunshot wound through his head. He was already dead. There was nothing anyone could have done.'

There was something I could have done. I could have been home when he called me.

I chose not to dwell on that. I knew Travis had made his choice, and if I let myself feel guilty—if I blamed myself—I would never recover from it.

(Fast-forward about two and a half years.)

The winter of 1991–92 was one of the snowiest in Idaho history. It was Christmas break, and a blizzard was raging. I was staying at home during the break, but my job at the Rexburg Nursing Center was 20 miles away. I had considered skipping work that day, but I knew what it was like to work short-handed, and knew it wasn't fair to the other nursing assistants I worked with, so I finally decided to brave the weather.

The road was white with snow piled at least three feet high on both sides, with more snow blowing around furiously. It appeared that it was all focused right at me. Even at full blast, the windshield wipers couldn't keep up with the snow blowing at the car. I had the heater on high trying to defog the windows, and the radio blasting to provide a feeling of security.

I knew that once I got on the freeway, I'd be fine, but I was concerned about safely getting onto it. The country roads were covered in ice and snow and there was a train track coming up. The road raised to go up over the tracks and then down onto the freeway. If I wasn't careful, the hill would be a slippery slope and I would slide right into oncoming traffic on I-20. I was so focused on the freeway and the noise in the car was so deafening, I didn't see or hear the train coming.

The first thing I remember was I was in a hospital room, laying in a bed and Travis was sitting beside me. I wasn't afraid. This didn't seem unusual. Travis was teasing me about my driving skills—or lack thereof—and I felt completely calm. His familiar pleasant teasing proved to me that it really was he.

'Come with me, I want to show you something.' There was an excitement in his eyes, like the way he looked when we talked about catching lizards, but what he was about to show me was a lot cooler than any reptile.

Within a blink of an eye, we were no longer in the hospital room and Travis wasn't wearing jeans and a flannel shirt anymore. The place he had taken me was exquisitely white and everyone, including Travis, was wearing a white robe. There were thousands of people all heading in different directions. They seemed to be focused, but not in a hurry. I saw my grandma from a distance. She didn't stop, but I could feel her communicating with me. I felt all the love that she felt for me, and I remembered the special times we had spent together. It was almost like reliving them.

I didn't know where they were going or what they were doing, but I knew it was important and that there were other very good, very wise people, directing them. I knew one of them was my cousin Russell, a strong-willed toddler with a big personality who had died when he was two [our son].

My cousin Jamie, who was close to my age and had died a few years earlier in a motorcycle accident came up to us and talked to me, using his voice. He reminded me of a dream I had had about him shortly after he had died. At the time, the dream had scared me, but I felt strongly that it had meant something. Jamie assured me that my feelings had been legitimate and that the dream had something to do with what was going on right then as we spoke.

Jamie had died in the same wing of the hospital in which my unconscious body was lying. As hard as it was for his parents, they came to be there with my parents, comforting and reassuring them. After talking to Jamie, I knew it was not my time to go. Yet I would struggle to leave this place where the feeling of love was so strong. I had never felt anything like it before, and yet I knew exactly what it was. It was the love of my Savior, Jesus Christ, and my Heavenly Father. I realized it was a love that was stronger than any I could possibly comprehend if I hadn't been in this special place.

I did go back to the hospital room, but my body must have been asleep. The only thing I remember from the three weeks that my body was in a coma was that Travis was a frequent visitor. Every time he came, he took me to a different place.

The last place that Travis took me was the most beautiful. It was a lagoon encircled by waterfalls and surrounded by a grassy area. There were children playing in the grass and swimming in the water. Some were picking flowers. I felt like these children were the most precious souls that God had created, and I was honored and humbled to be in their presence. Without anyone saying anything to me, I knew these were my children. These were the spirits that I would have the privilege of raising as my own if I were to return to earth. I knew why I had been allowed to come to this place. I needed to go back, but I needed to go back strong, fighting to recover, if I were to have the blessings that were in store for me.

After three weeks, I came out of the coma. My dad had been cheering me on and advocating for me. My sister sat with me, played music for me, brushed my hair and made me feel somewhat normal. My mom made my journey feel like I was coming back to a stable place where I was loved and wanted. My brothers had sacrificed sports, and other typical high school activities. They had cleaned the house, done laundry, and gone grocery shopping so my parents could be with me.

I had suffered a head injury and it was difficult for me to communicate my feelings. I had experienced something remarkable, and I couldn't restrain my enthusiasm, but with my right side temporarily paralyzed and my teeth wired shut (broken jaw) I couldn't share the wonder of it all.

Travis's parents came in to visit me in the hospital. My heart was full! I wanted to make them understand, but the only words that would come to my mind were that Travis was okay. Travis was happy. Although there was a lot more I would have liked to explain, I knew that those were the things that it was most important to Travis for them to know. My sister tells me that I told them over and over, 'Travis is gone, but he's okay.'

NOTE

- Correspondences from Rachel Potter Andersen and Kristy Shaw Amrine are in the possession of the author.

Wesley M. White

Chapter 3
Through a Glass, Darkly

> "For now we see through a glass, darkly; but then face to face: now I know in part; but then shall I know even as also I am known."
> — *1st Corinthians 13:12*

By nature, we are concerned about the next life. We ponder questions such as: *Is there life after death? If so, what will it be like? What will be different? What will be the same?* I am extremely grateful for insight given to me years ago.

While I was serving as a stake president, a choice sister in the stake passed away. She had been valiant in mortality and faithful through severe health challenges. She inspired all who knew her.

The morning after her passing, I was awakened very early and taught by the Spirit, a rare and sacred experience. The first prompting was, "This is what I want you to teach at Sister ____'s funeral." Interestingly, I had not been asked to speak at her funeral. That request came later the same day.

I was taught that even though I had known this sister for many years, should I be allowed to visit her now, in paradise, I would know her better in just moments than I had during all our many years of mortal association. I was reminded of 1st Corinthians 13:12, "For now we see through a glass, darkly; but then face to face: now I know in part; but then shall I know even as also I am known."

In more modern language, we might say that in mortality, we see other mortals in a distorted view through many "filters." That morning I was taught about four of these filters.

First, in mortality we see every person in his or her fallen state. We see each person's weakness (see *Ether 12:27*) that comes with mortality. Some of this weakness is general to all mankind (fear, insecurity, carnal desires, pain, pride, illness, and such). But we also have our "personalized challenges" (depression, disability, anxiety, migraine headaches, and a myriad more) customized for each of us.[1]

As author and scholar C. S. Lewis wrote in *Mere Christianity*:

> Most of man's psychological make-up is probably due to the body; when his body dies all that will fall off of him, and the real central man, the thing that he chose, that made the best or the worst out of this material, will stand naked. All sorts of nice things which we thought our own, but which were really due to a good digestion, will fall off from us: all sorts of nasty things which were due to complexes or bad health will fall off others. We shall then, for the first time, see every one as he really was.[2]

Robert Hugh Benson, who is oft-quoted in this book and is the author of *Life in the World Unseen* (listed under Anthony Borgia, due to Benson relating it to Borgia), expressed it as follows:

> All these conditions [the stresses of mortality] bring with them a consequent infirmity of temper. Under the stress of such a life, we do not always appear at our best. We can become irritable, or cynical; we think we are possessed of all truth and inclined to regard as fools others who do not think as we do. We become thoroughly intolerant.[3]

He also stated that:

> [When] we leave all the worrying cares of the earth behind us . . . the beauties and charms of [the spirit world] act like an intellectual tonic; they bring out only that which is and always was the very best in one . . . we are no longer subject to the stresses that produce the unpleasant qualities that were observable in us when we were on the earth . . . . Our tempers [are] very often sorely tried in [our] days upon earth. [In the spirit world], we know [each other] as we really are.[4]

Perhaps Doctrine & Covenants (D&C) 76:94 references the same principle: "They shall see as they are seen and know as they are known."

Second, every person we know or see has the adversary nipping at his heels at every turn, particularly taking advantage of his mortal weaknesses. President Howard W. Hunter taught:

> When Jesus had completed the fast of forty days and had communed with God, he was, in this hungry and physically weakened state, left to be tempted of the devil.
>
> That, too, was to be part of His preparation. Such a time is always the tempter's moment—when we are weary, vulnerable, and least prepared to resist his insidious temptations.[5]

As with Jesus, so with us, relief comes, and miracles are enjoyed only after the trial and temptation of our faith.

Satan never rests from his efforts to allure us, tempt us, beguile us, and keep us from experiencing joy or strengthening others. His greatest success comes by kicking us when we are down.

Third, because we know each other only "through a glass, darkly," we often misunderstand others' motives. Perhaps the most well-known example of this is the hunter who returns to his cabin to the cries of his infant son. Seeing his dog's mouth covered with blood, he immediately grabs his ax and kills the dog. It is then that he notices a dead wolf in the cabin and realizes that the dog had protected his infant from the wolf.

Unlike that example, you may see humor in a misperception that once caused great embarrassment to my wife, Kay. It came early in my career as an Air Force pilot. The Yom Kippur war (1973) had just begun. My flying squadron put me on high alert and told me to report very early the next morning with personal necessities for ninety days.

Just minutes later, I received another call, this time from a man I had previously home taught but who had moved from the area. He said he was back in town and asked to stay with us. I explained that I was about to be deployed and only my wife and three small children would be home. He surprisingly answered, "That's okay," and came over!

When I reported to my squadron early the next morning, we learned that we were deploying to Israel to assist in the war. Now knowing the destination, I realized I had packed several things I wouldn't need. Another pilot's wife (who didn't have three little kids and company at home) had come to see her husband off. I asked her to take my unnecessary items to Kay.

When she arrived at our home, Kay was busy in the kitchen, and our uninvited guest answered the door. My associate's wife looked at him in disbelief for a moment and then asked for Kay. She gave Kay the things I had sent home and told her coldly, "The plane isn't even off the ground yet!" It was difficult for Kay to come up with an adequate explanation, but we still laugh about it.

Fourth, mortality by design, beats us up. We all bear many scars: emotional, spiritual, mental, or all three. For example, when I was a young missionary serving in Texas, I had adjusted to having a "24/7" companion, and my companions had somehow learned to endure me. However, one companion certainly challenged my patience.

He was a braggart but couldn't back up his wild claims. He told me repeatedly of his exceptional high school athletic ability, the winning basket, the home run to win the game, or the last-second touchdown, however, when we would gather for preparation day sports, he couldn't deliver. He lacked the athletic ability for his stories to be true. How that grated on my nerves! I'm sure my disgust showed in my disposition, but he seemed to respond with even more accounts of spectacular sports "accomplishments."

However, I received a tender mercy. While on exchange with another missionary, proselyting along a dusty Texas road, I aired my frustrations. The other elder listened patiently and then asked, "What do you know about Elder Jones' (not his real name) background?" The question seemed irrelevant to my frustrations, but I allowed him to continue. He explained that he was from the same small town as Elder Jones, and he began to describe Elder Jones's life, although I must admit that at first, I wasn't interested.

I learned that Elder Jones was born near the end of World War II, while his father was off to war. In fact, Elder Jones' conception happened while his "father" was gone. Elder Jones' mother knew she should write and tell her husband, but she didn't gather the courage until shortly before he returned.

Coming home to a son that he didn't father hit him hard. Elder Jones' "parents" tried to patch things up, but it was tough. Frequent arguments evolved into trying to hurt the other ever more deeply. His mom's infidelity and the resultant son became the father's ultimate weapon. He would point to the child and say to his wife, "Look at what you did to me while I was off to war!"

The family relationship deteriorated to the point that Elder Jones was sent to live with relatives. However, he was no more loved in this new environment than in the old. In some ways, this environment was even worse.

As I listened to Elder Jones' story, my picture of him completely changed, as did my attitude. He immediately went from "zero to hero." My frustration was gone, replaced by respect—in fact, awe. I marveled that, having come from such a background, he was on a mission. When he boasted, I understood. I earnestly tried to make him feel better about himself from then on. It turned out, to know him was to love him.

Though Elder Jones' case may be exceptional, none of us is free from mortality's severe buffetings. To a degree, all of us suffer from some type of post-traumatic stress. The effects show on us, but the causes generally go unknown. What a blessing it was for me to learn about Elder Jones' "scars."

Robert Hugh Benson explained it this way:

> [When] we leave all the worrying cares of the earth behind us . . . the beauties and charms of [the spirit world] act like an intellectual tonic; they bring out only that which is and always was the very best in one . . . we are no longer subject to the stresses that produce the unpleasant qualities that were observable in us when we were on the earth . . . .
>
> Our tempers [are] very often sorely tried in [our] days upon earth. [In the spirit world] we know [each other] as we really are.[5]

Perhaps D&C 76:94 references the same principle: "They shall see as they are seen and know as they are known."

And finally, we see others "through a glass, darkly" not only because of their fallen state, Satan's efforts, and their scars, but also because of our fallen state. We prejudge others for their national origin, race, color, disposition, age (young or old), religious beliefs, sports-team affiliation, physical stature, and hundreds (maybe thousands) more. No wonder the scriptures counsel us to "watch" (perhaps looking for the beam in our own eye) and to "pray always" (*Matthew 26:41*), as well as warn us to "judge not" (*John 7:24*), reserving final judgment to Christ Himself.

So here we are, fallen, tempted, misunderstood, and scarred, but a loving Heavenly Father and Jesus Christ, together with the third unembodied member of the Godhead, the Holy Spirit, unite to provide a way to paradise after death and a pathway to a celestial eternity for all who merit it. It is their work and their glory, and they have "no distracting hobbies."[6]

Because of His divine nature, the Lord will maximize mercy and minimize punishment. President J. Reuben Clark said it this way:

> I feel that [the Savior] will give that punishment which is the very least that our transgression will justify.
> I believe that he will bring into his justice all the infinite love and blessing and mercy and kindness and understanding which he has ... And on the other hand, I believe that when it comes to making the rewards for our good conduct, he will give us the maximum that it is possible to give, having in mind the offense which we have committed.[7]

In summation, by suffering the excruciating Atonement, the Savior overcame "the world" (*John 16:33*) and everything associated with it. Therefore, through our faithfulness and His Atonement on our behalf, we can be free of the weaknesses of mortality, the temptations of Satan, and the scars of this life.

Although I don't know how the Savior's Atonement applies to those who die and don't attain paradise, the performance of vicarious temple ordinances proves that the Atonement is still active on their behalf. Although the road may be challenging, "scarlet" sins can "be as white as snow" (*Isaiah 1:18*).

Spirit World Basics

As we begin our examination of the next life, four basic teachings from Elder Neal A. Maxwell concerning the spirit world provide an introduction (and should perhaps also be dog-eared).

First, it is vast. He points out that demographers estimate that 60 to 70 billion people have now lived on this planet.

Second, the "sweat of thy brow" principle will not exist. Although we will be busy, the mundane chores of this world will not dominate our time as they do in mortality.[9]

Third, the spirit world is much more a "house of order" than is mortality.[10]

Fourth, the spirit world is like the second estate in that the plan of salvation is still active and the veil of forgetfulness that prevents us from having a perfect knowledge and understanding of all things is still in place. There may be atheists in the spirit world, Elder Maxwell admits, but the principle of faith and the requirement to practice that faith through continued learning and progression will still apply there.[8]

NOTES

1. Maxwell, Neal A., "Endure it Well," General Conference, April 1990.
2. Lewis, C. S., *Mere Christianity*, 71. Lewis was perhaps the premiere Christian theologian of his day. He was British and taught at both Cambridge and Oxford. Until age 32, he called himself an atheist, but after being influenced by George MacDonald, J. R. R. Tolkien, Rudyard Kipling, and others, he became an ardent follower of Christ. He authored more than thirty books (including *The Chronicles of Narnia*), most of them resting in powerful prose and symbolism of Christ.
3. Borgia, Anthony, *Here and Hereafter*, 123.
4. Ibid., 110.
5. Hunter, Howard W., "The Temptations of Christ," General Conference, October 1976.
6. Maxwell, "How Choice a Seer!" General Conference, October 2003.
7. Faust, James E. "The Atonement: Our Greatest Hope," (quoting J. Reuben Clark) General Conference, October 2001.
8. Maxwell, *The Promise of Discipleship*, 105.
9. Ibid, 106.
10. Ibid, 110.

Chapter 4

Was the Length of Our Life on Earth Set Before Our Birth?

> "I have acquired a deep trust that my earthly existence is according to His will. I trust Father in Heaven has a plan for me, including the length of my mortal life. I promised in the spirit world to be obedient to His plan. Therefore, I need not fear."
> — *Rachel Andersen*

Oh, this thing we call death! It may take us within an instant of our birth or delay until our years of mortality have extended into triple digits. Anna, an elderly temple worker mentioned in the New Testament, is a scriptural example of the latter. She was one of the first to recognize the infant Jesus Christ as the long-anticipated Messiah. Gospel author Luke informs us that her husband had lived only seven years into their marriage, and that she had been widowed for 84 years (see *Luke 2:36–7*.) Some in their youth, who resonate with life and energy, are taken in a moment. Others of advanced age may yearn for death but linger for decades.

Is the duration of our lifetime random or foreordained? Elder Richard G. Scott of the Quorum of the Seventy wrote, "We will live for our appointed life span."[1] Ecclesiastes 3:2 states, "*[There is] a time to be born, and a time to die.*"

In his booklet *Tragedy or Destiny?*, President Spencer W. Kimball taught, "I am confident that there is a time to die, but I believe that many people die before 'their time' because they are careless, abuse their bodies, take unnecessary chances, or expose themselves to hazards, accidents, and sickness."[2]

Author Lee Nelson tells of a woman about to die who said her deceased husband still loved her and wanted her to join him. "'When is he coming for you?' someone asked. She replied, 'In the morning, early.' She died the next day at 6:15 a.m."[3]

In writing of her NDE, author Betty J. Eadie, referring to children who die young, said, "I understood that their death had been appointed before their births—as were ours. These spirits did not need the development that would result from longer lives in mortality."[4]

Eadie also addressed violent death, "If our deaths are traumatic, the spirit quickly leaves the body, sometimes even before death occurs."[5]

I am particularly grateful for this last statement because several years ago I was asked to speak at the funeral of a dear friend's granddaughter, who had died in a fiery crash. I was prompted to say that her spirit left her body an instant before the accident. I had never heard such doctrine, so Eadie's words comforted me: I had probably responded to a valid prompting.

From the much pondering I have done since our young son died many years ago, I believe that a child who has not reached the age of accountability (which is eight years old, according to the Lord in *D&C 68:27*) will not die unless he or she is foreordained to do so. These little children cannot be tempted by Satan (see *D&C 29:47*), and they are not accountable for placing themselves in danger or even capable of recognizing many hazardous situations. Our God is a God of mercy as well as justice, and it seems to me to be unfair to take a child's life when he or she puts her/himself in peril and is not accountable for doing so—unless he was foreordained to a brief mortality.

Speaking of the death of children, Joseph Smith, the first prophet of the Church of Jesus Christ of Latter-day Saints, proclaimed:

> In my leisure moments, I have meditated upon the subject and asked the question, why is it that infants, innocent children, are taken away from us, especially those that seem to be the most intelligent and interesting . . . The Lord takes many away even in infancy, that they may escape the envy of man, and the sorrows and evils of this present world; they were too pure, too lovely, to live on earth; therefore, if rightly considered, instead of mourning we have reason to rejoice as they are delivered from evil, and we shall soon have them again.[6]

President John Taylor called these children "noble spirits" who could not be spared from important spirit world assignments for an extended time, so they were "furloughed" to a short mortal experience before resuming greater works.[7]

Further, the non-foreordained early death of a child would be unfair not only in mortality, but also in eternity. The child would miss choice opportunities to learn from the experiences only to be gained in mortality.

To the question, "are [children] automatically saved?" Elder Bruce R. McConkie replied:

> To this question the answer is a thunderous yes, which echoes and re-echoes from one end of heaven to the other. Jesus taught it to His disciples. Mormon said it over and over again. Many of the prophets have spoken about it, and it is implicit in the whole plan of salvation.

He added:

> We may rest assured that all things are controlled and governed by Him whose spirit children we are, although in deference to our moral agency. He knows the end from the beginning [*D&C 130:7*], and he provides for

> each of us the testing and trials which He knows we need . . . Joseph Fielding Smith [Elder McConkie's father-in-law] once told me that we must assume that the Lord knows and arranges beforehand who shall be taken in infancy and who will remain on earth to undergo whatever tests are needed in their cases.[9]

Many people who have experienced a near-death experience have said they did not want to return to the labors of earth life but were required to return because their "time" had not yet come. It is not possible for us to understand every aspect of the complex celestial equation of death, but we can, with certainty, say that there are no unanticipated arrivals into the next world.

Rachel Andersen, who relates her experience throughout this book, beginning in Chapter 2, wrote:

> My NDE has taught me of the temporary nature of earthly life. An ever-loving and all-knowing Father ultimately determines how long we spend in mortality. I have acquired a deep trust that my earthly existence is according to His will. I trust Father in Heaven has a plan for me, including the length of my mortal life. I promised in the spirit world to be obedient to His plan. Therefore, I need not fear.

NOTES

1. Scott, Richard E., "How to Obtain Revelation and Inspiration for Your Personal Life," General Conference, April 2012.
2. Kimball, Spencer W., "Tragedy or Destiny?" pamphlet, 9.
3. Nelson, Lee, *Beyond the Veil*, 141.
4. Eadie, Betty J., *Embraced by the Light*, 95.
5. Ibid., 95-96.
6. Smith, Joseph Fielding, *Teachings of the Prophet Joseph Smith*, 196-197.
7. Hill, Mary, *Angel Children*, 55.
8. *Doctrine and Covenants Student Manual*, 1981, 355.
9. Ibid.

Chapter 5

Does God Have a Particular Earthly Mission for Each of His Children?

> "My dear friends, premortally, you and I were each given wonderful missions to fulfill while here on earth."
>
> — *Sister Wendy Nelson*

We know that the premortal Jesus Christ volunteered to be the central figure in Heavenly Father's plan for His family. He, the Firstborn, was the only child of the Father advanced enough to do so. The role was not to eclipse the Father but to glorify Him, which is in striking contrast to Lucifer's proposal to "give me thine honor" (*Moses 4:1*). (Elder Maxwell pointed out that Satan said "I" four times and "me" twice in this one verse.)

The Son then offered, "Thy will be done," (*Moses 4:2*). He not only lived up to the Father's plan by paying the excruciating price of our sins, but He also died for them.

We know that others were given specific missions to fulfill in mortality. John the Baptist was born to be a forerunner to Christ, announcing Him to Israel. Moses was born to lead the children of Israel out of bondage, and Joshua to establish them in the promised land. Years later, the Virgin Mary's mission was announced to her by the angel Gabriel.

Could it be that each of us is given a mission for this life? Few of us will have our missions laid out as plainly, but several NDEers testified that the Lord's universe is a house of order, on both a grand and an individual scale.

With the personal experience gleaned from her own NDE, author Betty Eadie testified, "I saw that we all volunteered for our positions and stations in the world."[1]

More recently, President Russell M. Nelson's wife, Wendy, gave an address in a worldwide youth devotional where she and her husband—the prophet—spoke. She strongly espoused foreordination:

> So, let me ask you a question: What were you born to do? . . . How I wish you could watch a 10–minute video of your premortal life on YouTube . . . If you could see yourself courageously responding to attacks on truth and valiantly standing up for Jesus Christ, I believe that every one of you would have the increased power, increased commitment, and eternal perspective to help you overcome any and all of your confusion, doubts, struggles, and problems. All of them!
>
> If you could remember who you said you would help while you are here on earth or what anguishing experiences you agreed to go through, that whatever really tough situation you are presently in—or will be in—you would say, 'Oh, now I remember. Now I understand. This difficult situation makes sense to me now. With the Lord's help I can do this!' . . . I like to imagine that each of us came to earth with a scroll attached to our spirits entitled *Things to Do While on Earth* . . . My dear friends, premortally, you and I were each given wonderful missions to fulfill while here on earth.[2]

In a similar vein, Eadie taught:

> There are far fewer accidents here than we imagine, especially in things that affect us eternally. The hand of God, and the path we chose before we came here, guide many of our decisions and many even seemingly random

experiences we have. It's fruitless to try to identify them all, but they do happen, and for a purpose. Even experiences such as a divorce, sudden unemployment, or being a victim may ultimately give us knowledge and contribute to our spiritual development. Although these experiences are painful, they can help us grow . . . Under the guidance of the Savior, I learned that it was important for me to accept all experience as potentially good.[3]

Our prayers therefore should include President Nelson's injunction, "Let God prevail" (General Conference, October 2020—General Conference is held twice a year in Salt Lake City and broadcast to members of the Church worldwide). We should then be on a constant lookout for opportunities to fulfill that mission—and be willing to change our personal agenda at any moment, if necessary.

Character Built Through Crisis

I learned something about very challenging mortal experiences enhancing one's character. I was an Air Force officer in 1973, when the American prisoners of war returned from Vietnam. It was one of the most touching and impactful events of my life. Some of our men had been held as long as seven and a half years.

All had been incarcerated with inadequate clothing, food, and medical care. They were brutally tortured, some to the brink of death. Most remained true to our country under terrible circumstances, and they still carry the physical and emotional scars from the experience.

After their release, they were not ready to immediately integrate back to their military professions. As part of their healing process, many Air Force ex-POWs were sent on extensive lecture tours to Air Force bases around the world. I was privileged to hear several of them speak.

The POW experience influenced each one of them differently. Some said they now knew there was no God. Others stated, just as strongly, that they now knew there is a God.

Almost all of them said, however, that although they would never want to go through the experience again, they were glad it had happened to them. They reported that they learned life-changing things that they could not have learned in any other way. They were better men for what they had suffered.

In my mind, their expression is a microcosm of our mortal lives. I believe that after we die and pass through that veil which separates us from the afterlife, we will recall many trials of mortality that we would never care to suffer again, but, at the same time, we will be grateful for such experiences. We will recognize each as having been essential to the development of our eternal character.

An Orderly Universe

Dr. Mary C. Neal, author of *To Heaven and Back*, learned from her NDE that there is much more order, and much less chaos, in this life than we are allowed to perceive:

> I remember a well-quoted analogy. We, as single threads, spend our lives worrying about our thread—what color it is and how long it is—even being upset if it becomes torn or frayed.
>
> The complete tapestry is far too large for us to see, however, and of too complex a pattern for us to appreciate the importance of a single thread. Regardless, without our individual contribution, the tapestry would be incomplete and broken.[4]

As Dr. Neal alluded and Dr. Raymond Moody observed, '[many] NDEers come back with a sense that everything in the universe is connected. He tells of a no-nonsense businessman who reported: "One big thing I learned when I died was that we are all part of one big, living universe. If we think we can hurt another person or another living thing without hurting ourselves, we are sadly mistaken. I look at a forest or a flower or a bird and say, 'that is me, part of me.'"[5]

Dr. George Ritchie expressed it this way: "He has created an extremely orderly universe, which operates as a result of definite laws and principles."[6]

Our Tailor-Made Trials

Brigham Young wrote, "Every trial and experience you have passed through is necessary for your salvation."[7] Similarly, President Gordon B. Hinckley stated:

> All must pass through a 'refiner's fire,' and the insignificant and unimportant [events] in our lives can melt away like dross and make our faith bright, intact, and strong. There seems to be a full measure of anguish, sorrow, and often heartache for everyone, including those who earnestly seek to do right and be faithful. Yet this is a part of the purging to become acquainted with God.[8]

David S. Baxter, a member of the Quorum of the Seventy, taught that "our character is shaped in the crucible of affliction."[9]

President Harold B. Lee said:

> Some of us have been tried and tested until our very heart strings would seem to break. I have heard of people dying with a broken heart, and I thought that was just a sort of poetic expression, but I have learned that it could be a very real experience. I came near to that thing, but when I began to think of my own troubles, I thought of what the apostle Paul said of the Master, 'Though he were a Son, yet he learned obedience by the things which he suffered; and being made perfect, he became the author of eternal salvation unto all them that obey him' (*Hebrews 5:8-9*).
>
> Don't be afraid of the testing and trials of life. Sometimes when you are going through the most severe tests, you will be nearer to God than you have any idea, for like the experience of the Master himself in the tempta-

tion on the mount in the Garden of Gethsemane, and on the cross at Calvary, the scriptures record, 'And behold angels came and ministered unto him' (*Matthew 4:11*). Sometimes that may happen to you in the midst of your trials."[10]

A friend and neighbor, Ryan Rampton, experienced an NDE and subsequently wrote a book about it. He concludes:

> God has created a perfect plan for your life. Just like each fingerprint is different, and each snowflake is different and unique, your life was designed by God and your highest self to create the perfect path for your learning. This is how much God values you . . . Imagine the beauty of each unique individual. God loved you enough to create an individual plan for your growth and happiness. I testify how much he loves you, and how unique and special you are to him. I pray that you will begin to see yourself as God sees you.[11]

Some years ago, a member of our stake was driving to Salt Lake City on a cold winter morning when her automobile hit a patch of ice. She lost control of her car and also lost her life, leaving her husband with six children, aged 18 months to 13 years.

When I met with her husband a few months later, the Spirit whispered to me that we as mortals cannot even begin to understand how eternally important it is that this brother was remaining true to the covenants he made in the temple under such trying circumstances. Like the POWs who were grateful for their experiences, I believe this faithful brother, when he meets the Savior and reviews his life, will be grateful for his experience as he receives an "exceedingly great reward" (*Genesis 15:1*).

President Gordon B. Hinckley summarized his outlook on the challenges of life when, at the age of 83, he wrote, "I have experienced my share of disappointments, of failures, of difficulties, but on balance, life has been very good."[12] May we emulate his outlook.

Rachel's Experience

I believe I not only agreed but was also willing and eager to participate in my NDE before coming to earth. As time passes, I become more certain of this. For I would not, could not, have the life I have been blessed with presently if not for my NDE.

Most obvious is my choice of an eternal companion. It was through much fasting and prayer that Brian received a lifetime testimony of Christ and of His gospel. Upon our continued faith and obedience, the highest of blessings of eternal family is now obtainable. This evidence proves to me that I knew and approved of my great challenge prior to earthly life. Pres. Joseph F. Smith observed how ... we often catch a spark from the awkward memories of the immortal soul, which lights up our whole being as with the glory of our former home.' Thus, when we say, 'I know' that realization is rediscovery: we are actually saying 'I know—again.' We agreed to come here and to undergo certain experiences under certain conditions.

NOTES

1. Eadie, Betty J., *Embraced by the Light*, 53.
2. Nelson, Wendy, "Sister Wendy Nelson's Remarks," Worldwide Youth Devotional, June 3, 2018.
3. Eadie, 68-69.
4. Neal, Mary C., *To Heaven and Back*, 102.
5. Moody, Raymond, *The Light Beyond*, 4.
6. Ritchie, George, *Return from Tomorrow*, 14.
7. Widtsoe, John, *Discourses of Brigham Young*, 345.
8. Hinckley, Gordon B., "Faith in Every Footstep," Ensign, January 1997.
9. Baxter, David, "Faith, Fortitude, and Fulfillment," General Conference, April 2012.
10. BYU Press, *Teachings of Presidents of the Church: Harold B. Lee*, 58.
11. Rampton, Ryan, *You Were Born a Warrior: A Near Death Experience*, last paragraph.
12. Hinckley, Gordon B., "Some Lessons I Learned as a Boy," General Conference, April 1993.

Wesley M. White

Chapter 6

The Most Common Near-Death Experiences

> "I was shown events in my life, not in isolation but in the context of their unseen ripple effects. It is easy for us all to see the impact our words or actions may have on our immediate surroundings, but to see the impact of events or words dozens of times removed was profoundly powerful."
> — *Mary C. Neal*

This chapter commences the apex of our study of the spirit world. It merits some background. Throughout history, there have been many accounts of those who have visited the spirit world after death. Some of these date back thousands of years. Because of medical advances that allow physicians to resuscitate patients with flat EEGs and EKGs (patients who were clinically dead), these accounts now number in the tens of thousands. One would think that reports of this number would provide a clear understanding for the general population as to the existence and characteristics of what some refer to as the "next world." This is not the case. The problems of recording, classifying, and analyzing the huge number of late twentieth/early twenty-first century accounts are many. I have tried to do much of that labor for you.

Here, then, is a compilation of greatly abridged accounts of what comes between death and our final judgement. These experiences were confirmed by other researchers, then by official organizations, such as the Near-Death Experience Research Foundation (NDERF) and are a few of the most common. How exciting that [God] "will yet reveal many great and important things pertaining to the Kingdom of God" (*Articles of Faith #9, Pearl of Great Price*).

Out-of-Body Experiences

Many who had NDEs reported suddenly being above their body, looking down and watching their doctors' efforts to resuscitate them. Most reported a feeling of exceeding peace. In fact, some wished the resuscitation efforts would stop because they were feeling this transcending peace without discomfort of the body.

Many patients described in detail the surgical suite and its equipment—including gauges and the readings thereon—and the actions and comments of the surgical staff. In fact, one elderly lady, who had lost her sight years before, gave a detailed report of the operating room, what the equipment looked like, and where different people were standing. These were later verified by her physician.

Some patients even spiritually left the hospital and saw friends or relatives in distant places, describing their clothes, overheard conversations, and so on. To the surprise of these people, they related details they could not have known while under anesthesia, or in a state of clinical death.

Life Reviews

One NDE report by Vickie M. related:

> I felt as though I was looking down on myself for a brief moment, and then there was a real feeling of peace and calm. I was no longer scared or in pain.
>
> As my body hit the ground again, pictures of my life went through my mind. It was like a freight train of

knowledge moving at the speed of light. Each car carried experiences of my life (both good and bad), from the time that I entered my mother's womb until the present. I was the only one to judge my actions. I remember feeling so bad that I hit a frog with a stick as a young child. The last frame was a shot of seeing my husband with my two children, two and four years old.

After the life review, I heard my grandmother saying prayers over me, so I also said my prayers, 'Dear Lord Jesus, if you let me raise my kids, I will work for you the rest of my life, in your Son's name, Jesus Christ, amen.'[1]

And here is what Dr. Mary C. Neal recorded in her book *To Heaven and Back*:

As He held me, Jesus took me through a short review of my life. If I had any preconceptions about death, it would have been to assume that a life review would be the stereotypical image of one's life flashing before their eyes.

That is not what my experience was. I was shown events in my life, not in isolation but in the context of their unseen ripple effects. It is easy for us all to see the impact our words or actions may have on our immediate surroundings, but to see the impact of events or words dozens of times removed was profoundly powerful.

Through this experience, I was able to clearly see that every action, every decision, and every human interaction impacts the bigger world in far more significant ways than we could ever be capable of appreciating.[2]

Passing Through a Tunnel

From Victor Z. Sobes' near-death experience:

Then I felt like I was flying through some kind of dark tunnel.

Insofar as I had already heard about this on American broadcasts and read about it in local papers, I was not surprised, but rather expected it for some reason. I picked up tremendous speed. Such speeds are not encountered in life. My speed increased gradually, yet very quickly.[3]

Meeting a Loving Being of Light

Some NDEers humbly rejoice and delight about the time they spent with the Savior Jesus Christ during their NDE. An important observation came from Dr. Ritchie's NDE. After exulting from being with "Christ," he then noted that not everyone who professes the presence of Christ has been in the presence of the Savior himself. Dr. Ritchie explains that some spirits have so successfully emulated Christ that they are mistaken for Him.[4] The apostle John, speaking to the ancient saints made a similar declaration, that "when he shall appear, we shall be like him, for we shall see him as he is" (*1 John 3:2*).

Some NDEers identify this superior being with a great leader in their particular faith, but we learn from Ritchie that these religious leaders have come to know Christ and have emulated Him. It is noteworthy that in some of these experiences, the NDEer verbally declares this personage to be the Christ, but in all my research, not one of these personages declares being Him. In each case, the personage neither confirms nor denies being Christ.

William Si's NDE provides an example of this common event:

> The bright light had slowly transformed into a figure dressed in a white robe. Everybody became silent as the figure came towards me. The face of the figure was very bright, smiling and calm. I could even feel its warmth . . . asked, 'Are you God or Jesus?' I received a smiling response, 'William, not yet, go back, go back.' I said that I wanted to stay with my Father. I was told, with a shaking of the head, 'William, William, not yet, you have to go back.'
>
> [I was] physically, spiritually and consciously, extremely alert. To the point that I vividly recall all I saw and the conversations I had with those on the other side . . . it was real. The only thing I have to add to this is, while I was in my experience, I had the pleasure of having a discussion with Jesus. I knew it was Him and that, I can

never deny. I also received a wonderful hug from Him. I felt His body with my spirit, and there are times, especially when I do have occasional bouts of depression, I can still feel His physical body with my fingertips, and I know He was real and that what He brought to the world was wonderful.[5]

Seeing Deceased Relatives

From Mandy J.'s near-death experience:

First, there was an incredibly bright light . . . When I was finally able to adjust my eyes to the light, I looked around and I was in a beautiful area that was huge (maybe five to eight football fields in size). The grass was all green, the area smelt of roses and other flowers and there were rows of people being greeted by other people (spirits) that had died and gone before us.

I looked to my right and to my left then I looked in front of me and there were all my relatives and friends that had died, standing in the order they had died. For example, my Grandfather Lupe was the first person I remember dying (he died in 1955 when I was 10 years old), so he was the first person in line on the left side. These were only people that I loved and cared about deeply that had passed on before me.

On the right side was my grandmother (she passed on in 1991 at 92 years old). She was the first person I talked to, and I asked her, 'Grandma, why are you over there and not on this side with all the other people?' She was sitting in her green chair that she loved so much, and she was doing something with her hands. Possibly she was crocheting—because she loved to crochet but had not been able to crotchet in her last few years because of her eyesight. She looked up at me and, in Spanish (my grandmother spoke very little English) told me I have a little bit more to do, then I will go with the rest of them.

I turned back to my grandfather and told him how much I had missed him and how happy I was to see him. There were about twelve people in that line. I spoke with each and every one of them briefly, but had a longer discussion with my Uncle Donald, my dad's brother who drowned in 1989 (he was about 60 years old). I spoke with him, and he told me to give his brother Joe a message . . . .

At that time, I felt that I wanted to be in the warmth and comfort of these family members, and I decided I was going to cross over when my grandfather put his hand up and said, 'No, you can't come yet.' I asked, 'Why not?' He did not say a word, only looked up and I looked up to see what he was seeing. I can't even describe what it was, but I guess in order to put it into words I would have to say [that] in the sky, above this multitude of people-spirits, was The Father, The Son, and The Holy Ghost. I have been a Catholic all my life and didn't really understand what the three-in-one meant, but I do now.[6]

With these common experiences as a backdrop, we are ready to address the various realms of our next life.

NOTES

1. "Vickie M." NDE, NDERF, www.nderf.org/nderfexplorer/nderf_.html, retrieved January 10, 2022.
2. Neal, Mary C., *To Heaven and Back*, 57.
3. "Victor Z. Sobes," NDERF, www.nderf.org/nderfexplorer/ndeerf_.html, retrieved January 10, 2022.
4. Ritchie, *Ordered to Return*, 173.
5. "William Si NDE,", NDERF, www.Nderf.org/nderfexplorer/nderf_.html, retrieved January 10, 2022.
6. "Mandy J.," NDERF, www.nderf.org www.nderf.org/nderfexplorer/nderf_.html, retrieved January 10, 2022.

Chapter 7
Progress in the Spirit World

> "There are many levels of development, and we will always go to the level where we are most comfortable."
> — *Betty J. Eadie*

Some scientists estimate that more than a hundred billion people have already taken the step from mortality to the next life, yet we know so relatively little about the destination. We know that the mortal body remains in the grave and that our spiritual "self" moves on, fully alive, beginning the next step of potential eternal progression.

The individual spirit is the major part of what you feel in someone's personality. It is seldom made visible to humans. However, those who have experienced an NDE describe it as real to them as the mortal body during earth life. At the same time, those who have had an NDE struggle to describe it.

In a totally distinct (though correlated) world, there are just no adequate mortal words. Some say that the spirits and their world are composed of finer, more pure material than the mortal world, while others describe it as a different "frequency" than mortality. Perhaps the words "dimensions" or "planes of existence" could be helpful.

Ironically, we will begin examining the spirit world by dispelling three falsehoods: First, that there is no life after death;

second, that the next life is composed of solely heaven/paradise or hell/hades; and third, that death impedes opportunities for the spirit to progress. The first correction is easy—this entire book testifies to continuing life after death.

Dispelling the second misunderstanding, President Brigham Young taught that there are multiple spirit world "departments,"[1] (we will call them "realms") and the Church published this truth to all the world in *Teachings of Presidents of the Church: Brigham Young*, a Priesthood/Relief Society manual (© 1997). President Young explains that at the end of our mortal existence, we temporarily lay our body aside and enter a realm of the spirit world.

At President Jedediah M. Grant's funeral in December 1856, President Heber C. Kimball quoted President Grant, who had visited the spirit world two consecutive nights before his death. He stated that President Grant saw the spirits "organized in their several grades," and that he saw "grade after grade."[2]

In a similar vein, Parley P. Pratt, an early Apostle of the Church, wrote, "in the Spirit World there are many levels of good and evil."[3]

How many realms there are is not known with certainty. Brent and Wendy Top, in their book *Glimpses Beyond Death's Door*, said the visionary Emanuel Swedenborg (1688–1772) wrote about visiting three levels in the spirit world.[4] Ritchie reported visiting five.[5] The Savior stated, 'In my Father's house are many mansions" (*John 14:2*).

Monsignor Robert Hugh Benson, an Anglican priest, son of the Bishop of Canterbury, and author of the book *Confessions of a Convert*, said there were seven major realms.[6] Interestingly, some ancient Mesopotamian religions, including Judaism, Islam, and Christianity, taught that the next life is composed of "seven heavens."[7]

Regardless of the number of realms, when we pass from this life, we will gravitate to the realm where we fit according to how we have lived our life and what we have become.

Said Betty Eadie, "There are many levels of development, and we will always go to the level where we are most comfortable."[8]

Third, death is in many respects a graduation to greater opportunity for progress across a broad spectrum. Brigham Young plainly taught that spirits can progress from "department to department."[9] Monsignor Benson also taught that spirits can progress to higher realms: "The high spheres are within the reach of every…soul." He further explains that: "Every spirit residing in the lower realms hates the unhappiness there . . . [However, under God's direction], "great organizations exist to help every, single soul who is living in them to rise out of them into the light."[10]

President Boyd K. Packer taught in a General Conference address in October 1995:

> Some years ago, I was in Washington, D.C., with President Harold B. Lee. Early one morning he called me to come into his hotel room. He was sitting in his robe reading *Gospel Doctrine*, by President Joseph F. Smith (1838–1918), and he said, 'Listen to this! Jesus had not finished his work when his body was slain, neither did he finish it after his resurrection from the dead; although he had accomplished the purpose for which he then came to the earth, he had not fulfilled all his work.
>
> And when will he? Not until he has redeemed and saved every son and daughter of our father Adam that have been or ever will be born upon this earth to the end of time, except the sons of perdition. That is his mission. We will not finish our work until we have saved ourselves, and then not until we shall have saved all depending upon us; for we are to become saviors upon Mount Zion, as well as Christ. We are called to this mission.

This opportunity for spirit world progress is so important that I include the glorious example of a man who accepted Christ, applied the Atonement, and performed his part diligently to attain a better realm.

In Robert Hugh Benson's experience in the afterlife, he and his assistant Ruth were helping an 18-year-old named Roger in his transition to the next life. During his orientation, Roger, who had been a businessman in mortality, asked Ruth and Robert how they felt. Ruth replied:

> I don't see how we could feel any better than we do already. Perhaps it's all a matter of comparison."
>
> 'That must be it,' the man replied, 'and compared with what I once felt, it is perfection. It might be called 'Paradise regained' if I were at all sure that I ever had it to lose and regain. But come inside, and let our new friend see what a spirit world country cottage looks like.
>
> This small dwelling was as neat and trim inside as it was outside, and everything was arranged with the greatest taste and refinement, and yet with an eye on solid comfort and enjoyment. In the apartment that we entered directly from the garden, the furniture was of ancient style, well-constructed and pleasant to behold. It was kept in a high state of polish and reflected the large bowls of flowers that were everywhere displayed. The other two rooms, both upstairs and down, were similarly appointed, and altogether the whole dwelling revealed the natural pride and devoted care of its owner.
>
> The tenant then began to rehearse his story. 'I have no shame in telling you, Roger, my friend, that this is a very different place from the one I inhabited when I first came into the spirit world, as Ruth and Monsignor Benson will tell you, and of course, Edwin.'
>
> 'Where is Edwin now? Why isn't he with you?'
>
> 'He has been very busy of late,' Ruth replied, 'and none of us has seen much of him beyond a fleeting visit.'
>
> 'Roger is one of our own cases—do you like being referred to as a case, Roger? . . . we thought we would take time off and show . . . [Roger] things.'

'Doing for him, what Edwin did for you and Monsignor Benson,' he replied. 'Do you remember your first visit to me?—but of course you do. I shall never forget it.'

Ruth: 'If you feel so disposed, tell Roger about it.'

'Why, yes, if you wish, but he should know first how I came to live in such a place, such an awful place, as that was.

'When I lived on earth, Roger, I was a successful businessman. Business was my preoccupation in life, for I thought of precious little else, and I considered all means right in my dealings with others, provided such means were strictly legal. As long as they were that, I deemed the rest did not matter. I was ruthless, therefore, in gaining my ends, and coupled with a high degree of efficiency, I achieved great commercial success.'

'In my home, there was only one person to be thought of, and that was myself. The rest of the family did as they were told—and I did the telling.'

'I always gave generously to charity when I thought I should derive the greatest benefit and credit for myself, for I did not believe in anonymity as far as I was concerned. If any donations were to be given, I saw to it that my name was sufficiently prominent. Of course, I supported the church in the district where I lived, and at my own expense had some portions added to the building, with proper emphasis upon the donor.'

'The house I occupied was my own, and of such size and situation as befitted my position in the world. In every respect, Roger, I regarded myself as a god. It wasn't until I came to the spirit world that I discovered that I was one—made of tin, the sorriest, shabbiest god that ever existed.

'I was only a year or two past middle-life when disease overtook me, and at length, I died.

'I had every reason to know that I was given a magnificent funeral, with all the customary trappings, suitable mourning, and so on, though I have since learned that there was not a soul who cared a brass farthing that I had gone. On the contrary, they were glad. Some declared that the devil had got his own at last. Others said that I was the one justification for the existence of hell, and that the earth was sweeter for my removal. Such was the fragment memory I left behind me. And where was I, do you think, Roger, during all these sad lamentations at my departure?

'I awoke to find myself in the dirtiest, wretchedest hovel you can imagine. I could take and show you the place this moment, for it's still standing. The house—the hovel—was small, and seemed all the more so after the large establishment I was accustomed to on earth. It stood in a horrible, bleak spot, without garden or any living thing round about. The inside was in keeping with the outside, poorly, meanly furnished.

'Seeing it for the first time, some might have thought that poverty was the trouble. So it was—poverty of the soul—for I had never done anything for anyone on earth, except it be for my own ultimate benefit, not theirs.

'The very clothes I was wearing were threadbare and soiled. In the dingy hole I found myself, smoldering with rage that I should, in some inconceivable fashion, have been reduced to such a state of squalor. I didn't seem able to leave the premises; I felt glued to the house. I gazed out of the windows, and could see nothing but barren ground, with a belt of mist not far away. A grim, dismal outlook, in a literal sense. I stormed and raved, and it was in this situation that Edwin found me.

'He came to me one day, and I treated him as I had been accustomed to treat those whom I considered my inferiors on earth. Now Edwin was the last person to be spoken to in that fashion. You've not met him, have you, Roger, my boy? A quiet, kind personality, but firm. He stood no nonsense from me, I can tell you, but in my then frame of mind he could make no headway.

'I was consumed with anger, an anger that was aggravated by the fact that I did not know whom to blame for my present situation. The last person I thought of blaming was myself. However, I found some measure of consolation in assigning the responsibility where I fancied the largest share of it should rest, and that was upon the Church, for I felt I had been misled. Had I not given generously to the Church, and had I not been led to believe that my donations, and they were upon a considerable scale, would stand me in very good stead when my time came to depart the earth? I considered I had been done a grave injustice, and that the Church, of which I regarded myself a most ornate pillar, had flagrantly misled me, and that I was called upon to pay for its mistake.

'To whom was I to turn in my difficulties? I was perfectly well aware of what had taken place; in other words, that I was dead. But the mere knowledge of that was of precious little use.

'I suppose that I must have emitted some kind of thought in request of assistance. Whatever it may be, I perceived a man coming towards the house, and that man was Edwin. It was the first of several visits he paid me, and every one with the same results. I was adamant. I was also extremely rude. But Edwin was not the sort to be intimidated by one such as me, and he gave me as good—better, in fact—as I gave him! He simply marched out of the house and left me when I became too intractable.

'At length he returned, but this time not alone, for he brought with him two friends (and another I had sometimes seen in the area), the same two friends who are looking after you, Roger—Monsignor [Benson] and Ruth.

'Glancing back now, I know that visit was the turning point. Ruth and Monsignor stood in my room, very discreetly in the background, while Edwin spoke to me. I began to feel a trifle less angry, and my eyes were continually drawn towards Ruth, when I had first glimmerings of light, if I may so express it.

'Ruth's presence served to remind me that I had a daughter of my own, though I had treated her equally abominably with the rest. There was no physical resemblance between Ruth and my daughter, it was one more of temperament, as far as I could judge. Whatever it was, I already began to feel differently. That, combined with all that Edwin had spoken to me on so many occasions, had its effect. After my visitors had gone, a terrible loneliness came over me, as well as deep, dark remorse, so intense that I cried aloud in my despair for Edwin's presence now, which I had so often spurned with contempt, for I had put in some good thinking.

'You can imagine my joy and surprise when I perceived Edwin coming towards the house almost upon the instant of my cry. I met him at the door, and as he would tell you himself, I was a changed man.

'The first thing I did was thank him for coming so expeditiously—and I was not accustomed to thanking people for anything. The next, was to apologize to him for all I had said and done to him. But he waved my words aside with a brilliant smile upon his face that clearly bespoke his great pleasure that, at last, I was on the way to being something very different from the inflated egoist and spiritual blackguard that I was when I arrived in the spirit lands.

'Edwin at once sat down with me and proceeded to discuss ways and means of getting me out of the hell hole that was my abode. A course of action was decided upon. Edwin did the deciding, for I put myself entirely in his hands, and for the present it was arranged that I should remain where I was for a brief while, and that I had but to call him and he would come.

'After he had gone, I gazed round upon my house, and in some extraordinary manner it seemed brighter than it was. It was unquestionably less dingy, and my clothes were less shabby, and that discovery helped me feel a great deal happier.

'I will not bore you with all the struggles, hard struggles, I had to make up for all that was past. It was hard work, but I never lacked friends. I don't need to look farther than this room to see two at least.

'Well, Roger, you see me now, as unlike my old self as day is to night, still working hard, and glad of it. My work? Why, doing for others what Edwin did for me—and for the same kind of people! It's easier to handle them when you have been one of them yourself.'[11]

    That quote was long, but the great gift of continued progress in the next life merits the extended attention. And, progress is not limited to one realm. It merits repeating what Benson taught: "The high spheres are within the reach of every…soul."

NOTES

1. BYU Press, *Teachings of Presidents of the Church: Brigham Young*, Priesthood/Relief Society manual, 282. The Teachings of Presidents of the Church series was the course of study for both the Melchizedek priesthood quorums and the Relief Society for several years. Chapters 37 and 38 deal with the spirit world.
2. Crowther, Duane S., *Life Everlasting: A Definitive Study of Life After Death*, 175.
3. Ibid., 247.
4. Top, Brent L. and Wendy C., *Glimpses Beyond Death's Door*, 53.
5. Ritchie, George G., *Ordered to Return*, 45.
6. Borgia, Anthony, *Life in the World Unseen*, 129.
7. Ritchie, *Return from Tomorrow*, 47.
8. Eadie, Betty J., *Embraced by the Light*, 83.
9. BYU Press, *Teachings of Presidents of the Church: Brigham Young*, Priesthood/Relief Society manual, 282.
10. Borgia, *More Life in the World Unseen*, 85.
11. Borgia, *Here and Hereafter*, 63-68.

Wesley M. White

Chapter 8
An Overview of Hell and the Other Low Realms

> "They live to 'party' and spend countless hours trying only to entertain themselves and satisfy their wants, which they will never fill because these pleasures are empty and have no lasting or eternal value. They do nothing to elevate mankind or contribute to the improvement of the world."
> — *Sarah LaNelle Menet*

Hell

As shown on our graphic on the last page of the Introduction, the lowest realm in the spirit world is hell, also known as the depths of hell. When we speak of the inhabitants of this horrible realm, we are not talking of someone who intentionally ran over his neighbor's cat. We're talking the very worst of mankind. Some are responsible for the suffering and death of hundreds of thousands, or even millions, of people. They have sold out to greed. They are sadists who delight in the suffering of others. They will inflict pain on anyone for their personal wealth and glory.

Much of the Christian world believes hell is the permanent abode of the wicked. Through revelation, however, members of The Church of Jesus Christ of Latter-day Saints understand that this hell is not permanent. As we learned in the previous chapter, those who abide here will progress (should they choose repentance and learning) to a higher spirit world realm, and will eventually—after their resurrection—inherit a kingdom of glory.

The following description of spirit world hell is graphic but comes from credible NDEs. Robert Hugh Benson taught:

> There are many parts of the spirit world [hell] that are a thousand times worse than anything that can be found in the earth world.[1] In fact, spirits from higher realms visit hell only when accompanied by "master" escorts especially trained to keep them safe.
>
> [Their] dwellings were nothing more than mere hovels. They were distressing to gaze upon, but it was infinitely more distressing to contemplate that these were the fruits of men's lives upon earth.[2]
>
> Our nostrils were first assailed by the most foul odors, odors that reminded us of the corruption of flesh in the earth world.[3]

Eben Alexander, a neurosurgeon, described the smell as "a little like feces, and a little like blood, and a little like vomit."[4]

In *Return from Tomorrow*, Dr. George Ritchie stated that:

> Their bodies presented the outward appearance of the most hideous and repulsive malformations and distortions, the absolute reflection of their evil minds . . . Their limbs were indescribably distorted and malformed, and in some cases their faces and heads had retrograded to the merest mockery of a human countenance. Others again we observed to be lying prone on the ground as though exhausted from undergoing torture, or because of expending their last remaining energy upon inflicting it, before they could gather renewed strength, to recommence their barbarities.[5]

As the inhabitants had sown, so had they reaped. "Ugliness of mind and deed can produce nothing but ugliness."[6] The sounds were in keeping with the awful surroundings, from mad raucous laughter to the shriek of some soul in torment—inflicted by others as bad as himself."[7]

An Overview of Hell and the Other Low Realms

Several other people who experienced NDEs visited this miserable realm. Not surprisingly, these observers identified the inhabitants as "vassals of the devil,"[8]...horrific beings that clutch and claw at others."[9]...hideous and grotesque, savage, as in mortal life,"[10] and "intent upon evil."[11]

Dr. Ritchie called them "the most frustrated, the angriest, the most completely miserable I had ever laid eyes on."[12]

They live in a gloomy, barren, hostile place, in a total absence of love.[13] They still carry the addictions they acquired in the flesh, locked in with their habits of hatred and lust. Dr. Ritchie described sexual abuses being performed in feverish pantomime: "Perversions I had never dreamed of were being vainly attempted all around us, accompanied by howls of frustration."[14]

Because its inhabitants have rejected the Savior's plea to go through the process of repenting that they may not suffer even as He, unless they come to Him and repent, they must pay the "uttermost farthing" (*Matthew 5:26*) for their sins.

Eternal laws of justice require either that we repent, come unto Him, and take advantage of the infinite price He paid, or we meet the demands of justice ourselves. There is no other way.

Not surprisingly, there is divine purpose even in these dreadful abodes. According to Ritchie:

> They [are] given the chance to realize two very important facts. One, you can only kill the physical body, not the soul. Two, only love, not hate, can bring them and others to true happiness. God does not forget them. They are still His children. Even in those awful dark regions where everything is of the foulest, there yet reside within every one of those unhappy souls that celestial element—call it the divine spark if you wish . . . It is from that microscopic gleam that progress will commence, though it may take thousands of years of earthly time before it shows the least sign of activity, of increasing.[15]

This "divine spark" must certainly be the Light of Christ.

To provide any possible assistance to these souls, Richie notes, "That entire unhappy plane was hovered over by beings ... of light."[16]

Benson explains:

> Those from the higher realms are continuously anxious to grasp them from this awful abode as soon as they are ready to change. The Lord's love and tender watch-care, therefore, are constantly over His children.[17]
>
> [Spirits from higher realms] penetrated into these Stygian realms to try to affect a rescue out of the darkness. Some had been successful, some had not. Success depends not so much upon the rescuer as upon the rescued. If the latter shows no glimmer of light in his mind, no desire to step forward on the spiritual road, then nothing, literally nothing, can be done. The urge must come from within the fallen soul himself. And how low some of them had fallen![18]

Again, hell is not eternal. In fact, the spirit world will end prior to Judgment Day. That day is preceded by universal resurrection. We will stand before God in our resurrected bodies to be judged. However, all sins must be paid for before that time, either by accepting Christ's atonement, repenting and following him, or by personal suffering for all of one's own sins (*Matthew 5:26*).

Other Low Realms

You may remember that Monsignor Benson was a son of the Bishop of Canterbury and also the author of numerous books and plays. Several things make him an exceptional source for this book.

- As the son of the highest-ranking theologian in England, he was trained in writing and observing. It is natural that he would compile thorough notes describing the spirit world.
- He visited several realms during his NDE.
- His works are in notable harmony with the Gospel.

- He had been exposed to several Christian religions and observed that their theology concerning the next life was not even remotely in harmony with what he observed in the spirit world. This made him hyper-critical of Christian churches. He reminds me of the Savior rebuking the scribes and Pharisees.

Benson said:

> There are those whose earthly lives have been spiritually hideous though outwardly sublime; whose religious profession designated by a Roman collar, has been taken for granted as being synonymous with spirituality of soul. Such people have been mocking God throughout their sanctimonious lives on earth where they lived with an empty show of holiness and goodness . . . .[19]

I love Benson's caveat to this statement:

> Never must it be supposed that those who, in the earth's judgment, had failed spiritually, are fallen low. Many such have not failed at all, but are, in point of fact, worthy souls whose fine reward awaits them there.[20]

Sarah LaNelle Menet, who experienced an NDE and is the author of *There Is No Death*, described lower-realm inhabitants this way:

> . . . someone who doesn't do anything meaningful while on earth. This person doesn't progress, help others, or care. In a way, he or she just takes up space, doing nothing worthwhile . . . They live to 'party' and spend countless hours trying only to entertain themselves and satisfy their wants, which they will never fill because these pleasures are empty and have no lasting or eternal value. They do nothing to elevate mankind or contribute to the improvement of the world.[21]

Benson notes that many who attained worldly fame and acclaim are consigned to a low realm:

> We should be appalled by the catalogues of names, well known in history, who are living deep down in these

noxious regions—men who have perpetuated vile and wicked deeds in the name of holy religion, or for the furtherance of their own despicable, material ends.[22]

These lower realms are partially divided according to their associated worldly nations and thus carry on many customs and even wear traditional dress, although it is really a "replica" of earthly clothing.[23] However, as one develops spiritually and gains more knowledge and is thus qualified to progress into higher realms, these cultural and national distinctions disappear.

"Ghosts"

Some spirits of the deceased are permitted to linger with the living. I don't know the whys or the hows. Maybe it's associated with the Savior's instruction, "For where your treasure is there will your heart be also. (*Luke 12:34*). Dr. Ritchie gives us some insights from his NDE. He tells of a female spirit who asked a mortal woman for a cigarette, "begged her in fact, as though she wanted it more than anything in the world."[24]

Of course, the mortals were completely unaware of these spirits. Ritchie saw a number of the deceased sprits in a bar, trying to grasp drinks that frustratingly passed right through their hands. He saw a very drunk mortal. The spirits could briefly take possession of his body and partake of the drunken sensation.

Elder Parley P. Pratt spoke of these post-mortal lingering spirits:

> Many spirits of the departed, who are unhappy, linger in lonely wretchedness about the earth, and in the air, and especially about their ancient homesteads, and the places rendered dear to them by the memory of former scenes.[25]

Sarah LaNelle Menet explained, "Mischievous spirits are the ones that haunt houses, knock things over, and make noises. Righteous spirits are not involved in such practices."[26] Benson said that these wicked spirits exult in the sin and wickedness of degenerate humanity. Many of them are seeking revenge for something that occurred at the same location during their mortal years.

A Warning to Us

Benson warns us of the influence of the spirits in these realms upon the mortal world:

> From the dark realms you will have wars and strife, unrest and discontent; you will have literature that is a disgrace to so-called civilization and music, even, that is an abomination of impure sounds, such sounds as would never exist for an instant of time in the [higher] realms.[27]

Interestingly, Samuel the Lamanite from the Book of Mormon proffered the same warning to the Nephite nation:

> Behold, we are surrounded by demons, yea, we are encircled about by the angels of him who hath sought to destroy our souls.[28]

This can be chilling to contemplate, but remember that the Lord has given us hope and encouragement: "In the world ye shall have tribulation: but be of good cheer; I have overcome the world" (*John 16:33*).

NOTES

1. Borgia, Anthony, *Life in the World Unseen*, 81.
2. Ibid., 82.
3. Ibid., 85.
4. Alexander, Eben, *Proof of Heaven*, 55.
5. Ritchie, George, G., *Return from Tomorrow*, 81.
6. Borgia, 133.
7. Ibid.
8. Top, Brent L. and Wendy C., *Glimpses Beyond Death's Door*, 179.
9. Nelson, Lee, *Beyond the Veil*, 151.
10. Crowther, Duane S., *Life Everlasting: A Definitive Study of Life After Death*, 146.

11. BYU Press, *Teachings of Presidents of the Church: Brigham Young*, Priesthood/Relief Society manual, 282.
12. Ritchie, 63.
13. Top, 167.
14. Ritchie, 63.
15. Ritchie, 66.
16. Ibid.
17. Borgia, 51.
18. Ibid., 83.
19. Ibid., 84.
20. Ibid.
21. Menet, Sarah LaNell, *There is No Death*, 98.
22. Borgia, 85.
23. Borgia, *More Life in the World Unseen*, 19.
24. Ritchie, 56.
25. Crowther, 236
26. Menet, 121.
27. Borgia, *Here and Hereafter*, 87
28. Helaman 13:37

Chapter 9
An Overview of Paradise and the Other Higher Realms

> "... eye hath not seen, nor ear heard, neither have entered into the heart of man, the things which God hath prepared for them that love Him."
> — *1st Corinthians 2: 9*

The higher realms of the spirit world merit a brief review of the intra-relationships of these realms:

- Each realm is invisible to the realms below it. Thus, faith is still necessary for progression, just as it is in mortality. Remember, the spirit world is in many ways a continuum of the probation and progression of mortality.
- Conversely, each realm is visible to the realms above it. Throughout the spirit world, the spirits in higher realms assist the spirits in lower realms to progress.

Paradise

As mentioned earlier, most Christian faiths believe that heaven and the spirit world are the same place. However, paradise is the highest of several realms where the most righteous reside prior to the final judgement, after which everyone will be assigned to one of the many levels within either the celestial, terrestrial, or telestial kingdom.

What we do know is that paradise, whether or not it includes sub-levels, is the highest spirit world realm, and inhabitants therein are apparently free of all the constraints associated with mortality or with the other realms. It appears that their only "bondage" or limitation is the absence of their physical bodies (*D&C 138:50*).

We are told that paradise is a place of rest. The term "rest" cannot be taken too literally, however, as residents there are busy in the Lord's work. Said Brigham Young, "[They] are just as busy in the spirit world as we are here. They can see us, but we cannot see them unless our eyes are opened." He then asks rhetorically, "What are they doing there? Preaching, preaching all the time, and preparing the way for us to hasten our work in building temples here and elsewhere."[1]

Dr. George Ritchie, speaking of the highest realm, described the inhabitants as "beings who had followed His teachings and were now [revitalized] into spiritual beings who were like Him when it came to love, light, and life."[2]

In teaching the early Saints about the spirit world, it sounds as if Brigham Young had his own personal NDE. Said he, "I have been near enough to understand eternity so that I have had to exercise a great deal more faith to desire to live than I ever exercised in my whole life to live."[3]

He continues:

> The brightness and glory of the next apartment is inexpressible. It is not encumbered so that when we advance in years we have to be stubbing along and be careful lest we fall down . . . .
> But yonder, how different! They move with ease and like lightening. If we want to visit Jerusalem, or this, or that, or the other place—and I presume we will be permitted if we so desire—there we are looking at its streets.
> If we want to behold Jerusalem as it was in the days of the Savior; or if we want to see the Garden of Eden as it was when it was created, there we are, and we see it

as it existed spiritually, for it was created first spiritually and then temporally, and spiritually it still remains. And when there we may behold the earth as at the dawn of creation, or we may visit any city we please that exists upon its surface . . . we shall have a measure of [H]is power . . . [We] enjoy life, glory and intelligence; and we have the Father to speak to us, Jesus to speak to us, and angels to speak to us, and we shall enjoy the society of the just and the pure who are in the spirit world . . . .

. . . the fallen spirits—Lucifer and the third part of the heavenly hosts that came with him, and the spirits of wicked men who have dwelt upon this earth, the whole of them combined will have no influence over our spirits . . . the rest of the children of men are more or less subject to them, and they are subject to them as they were while here in the flesh.

We have more friends behind the veil than on this side, and they will hail us more joyfully than you were ever welcomed by your parents and friends in this world; and you will rejoice more when you meet them than you ever rejoiced to see a friend in this life; and then we shall go on from step to step, rejoicing to rejoicing, and from one intelligence and power to another, our happiness becoming more and more exquisite . . . .

When we get through this state of being, to the next room, I may call it, we are not going to stop there. We shall still go on, doing all the good we can, administering and officiating for all whom we are permitted to administer and officiate for, and then go on to the next, and to the next, until the Lord shall crown all who have been faithful on this earth, and the work pertaining to the earth is finished, and the Savior, whom we have been helping, has completed [H]is task, and the earth, with all things pertaining to it, is presented to the Father.[4]

President Young also corroborates that the plan of salvation continues in our next life, "Jesus was the first man that ever went to preach to the spirits in prison, holding the keys of the Gospel of salvation to them. Those keys were delivered to Him in the day and hour that he went into the spirit world, and with them he opened the door of salvation to the spirits in prison."[5] ("Spirits in prison," to some degree, includes every realm short of paradise. Even spirits in wonderful higher realms are in "prison' in that there are limits to what they can do, when compared to paradise.)

Thankfully, spirit bodies do not tire (or worry or fuss). Now that's true rest.

The Higher Realms

Paradise is not the only kingdom of magnificence and joy. Robert Hugh Benson reported that although other higher realms fall short of paradise, residents still find greater joy, learning, and glory there than the mortal mind can even fathom.

In fact, most NDEers who have seen higher realms speak of paradise and these higher realms jointly. From the experiences of NDEers, we find that many activities such as recreation are there as well. He observed lakes with boats, games, and even a concert.[6]

At the beginning of a heavenly concert, Benson stated:

> Never have I experienced such a feeling of real, genuine enjoyment as came upon me at this moment. I was in perfect health and perfect happiness, seated with two of the most delightful companions . . . unrestricted by time or weather, or even the bare thought of them; unhampered by every limitation that is common to our [mortal] life."[7]

Benson also noted:

> Personages from those [higher] realms have more than astonished me with the accuracy of their foreknowledge of events that were to take place upon the earth-plane . . . those wise beings in the higher realms are in possession of all knowledge of what is transpiring on earth.[8]

In fact, the past, present, and future of the earth is constantly before them (*D&C 130:7*).

An Overview of Paradise and the Other Higher Realms

In these higher realms, surnames are not used. Benson states:

> There is at least one fixed order of names here, and that is with the names that are of purely spirit world origin; names that are formed or built up in accordance with rules.
>
> Each one of them has a distinct meaning and belongs to no earthly language. Names of that kind are given after they have been earned and are only to be obtained through beings of the highest realms.[9]

Referring to this difference of knowledge in the high realms from those in the lower, he taught:

> There is . . . an enormous amount of things that are not told them, [i.e., those in lower realms] not because they are deep secrets, but because [they] have much to learn first.
>
> The fact is, that with our necessarily limited knowledge and powers of comprehension, [spirits in lower realms] should fail to understand them in [their] present state of advancement. It is like your school books. You were obliged to start at the beginning. A peep at the end of them would reveal things far beyond your then capabilities, and so would convey no meaning whatsoever . . . We find we are none the worse off for not knowing the answers. Everything fits into its proper place in these lands, and none of us would be handicapped in our progression by lack of knowledge. The knowledge will be there at the right moment.[10]

The Amazing Visit

Benson and a few others were invited to make a visit to paradise under the guidance and protection of two elite spirits sent to chaperone them. He introduces us to the magnificent paradise dweller who sent the invitation. In his words:

> The illustrious personage, towards whose home in the high realms we were making our way, was known by sight to every soul in the realms of light.

> His wish was always treated as a command, and his word was law. The blue, white, and gold in his robe, evident of such enormous proportions, revealed the stupendous degree of his knowledge, spirituality, and wisdom. There were thousands who named him as their 'beloved master.' The principal among whom being the Chaldean, who was his 'right hand.' As to his special function, he was the ruler of all the realms of the spirit world, and he exercised collectively that function which the particular ruler of a realm exercised individually. All other rulers, therefore, were responsible to him, and he, as it were, united the realms and welded them into one, making them one vast universe, created and upheld by the Great Father of all.
>
> To attempt to define the immense magnitude of his powers in the spirit world would be to essay the impossible. Even if it were possible, understanding would fail. Such powers have no counterpart, no comparison even, with any administrative power upon the earth plane. Earthly minds can conjure up those individuals who ruled great kingdoms upon earth, who held sway over vast territories, it may be, who did so through fear alone, and where all who lived under him lived as serfs and slaves. No earthly king throughout the whole narrative of the history of the earth world ever presided over a state so vast as that presided over by this illustrious personage of whom I am speaking. And his kingdom is ruled by the great universal law of true affection. Fear does not, could not, exist in the minutest, tiniest fraction, because there is not, and cannot be, the slightest cause for it. Nor will there ever be. He is the great living visible link between the Father, the Creator of the Universe, and His children.[11]

Benson detailed how a spirit is allowed to visit a higher realm than he or she occupies. "There are two ways, and two ways only, of penetration into these lofty states. The first is through our own spiritual development and progression; the second is by special invitation from some dweller in those regions."[12] Benson visited by invitation of the illustrious personage.

Benson's entourage arrived at "the most magnificent building that the mind could ever contemplate."[13] Passing through the corridors, they "were greeted by the most friendly and gracious beings."[14]

When they came into their host's presence, he:

> ... thanked the [escorts] for bringing us to him ... we drew close to the window, and we could see beneath us a bed of the most magnificent white roses, as pure white as a field of snow, and which exhaled an aroma as exalting as the blooms from which it came. White roses, our host told us, were the flowers their host preferred above all others.[15]

He more fully describes the personage who invited him:

> His hair seemed to be as of bright golden light ... He looked to be young, to be of eternal youthfulness, but we could feel the countless eons of time ... that lay behind him ... When he spoke, his voice was sheer music, his laugh as a rippling of water, but never did I think it possible for one individual to breathe forth such affection, such kindliness, such thoughtfulness and consideration; and never did I think it possible for one individual to possess such an immensity of knowledge as is possessed by this celestial king. One felt that, under the Father of Heaven, he held all knowledge and wisdom ... We felt perfectly at home, perfectly at ease with him ... He spoke to each of us individually, displaying an exact acquaintance with all our concerns, collectively and individually ....
>
> Finally, he came to the reason for his invitation to us. [We] had visited the dark realms ... He thought that it would be in the nature of a pleasant contrast if we were to visit the highest realm ... And he had asked us to visit him in order to tell us himself that these realms, wherein we were now visiting, were within the reach of every soul that is born upon the earth-plane.[16]
>
> This magnificent host concluded the visit with a blessing upon us all, and with a smile of such affection, of such ineffable benignity, he bade us God-speed.[17]

Ritchie taught (as have several apostles), "God, in His nature, is much more forgiving, understanding and just than we as humans are able to comprehend." To emphasize His glory, Ritchie added, "The garden was extraordinarily beautiful, but everything paled in His presence." Ritchie continued:

> This was the most totally male Being I had ever met . . . This Person was power itself, older than time and yet more modern than anyone I had ever met . . . . This Presence was unconditional love. An astonishing love. A love beyond my wildest imagining. This love knew every unlovable thing about me . . . and accepted and loved me just the same.[18]

We end this amazing chapter with the words of Paul and then the Prophet Joseph Smith.

Paul: "... eye hath not seen, nor ear heard, neither have entered into the heart of man, the things which God hath prepared for them that love him" (*1st Corinthians 2:9*).

Joseph Smith: "Ye cannot yet behold with your natural eyes, for the present time, the design of your God concerning those things which come hereafter, and the glory which shall follow after much tribulation" (*D&C 58:3*).

Betty J. Eadie expressed that a brilliant light, brighter than the sun, radiated all around Him and that "Jesus Christ is the only door through which we can return."[19]

Colton Burpo, whose NDE at the age of four was included in the book *Heaven is for Real*, said simply, "Jesus told me that he died on the cross so we could go see his dad."[20] How well this child articulated the Savior's sacrifice that we might return to "my Father, and your Father." (*John 20:17*).

Stated Dr. Ritchie of the divine presence:

> There was mirth in the Presence beside me, now I was sure of it: the brightness seemed to vibrate and shimmer with a kind of holy laughter—not at me and my

silliness, not a mocking laughter, but a mirth that seemed to say that in spite of all error and tragedy, joy was more lasting still.[21]

May the time come for each of us to experience this ultimate encounter.

NOTES

1. BYU Press, *Teachings of Presidents of the Church: Brigham Young*, Priesthood/Relief Society manual, 272-3.
2. Ritchie, George G., *Return from Tomorrow*, 49.
3. Young, 283.
4. Ibid.
5. Ibid.
6. Borgia, Anthony, *Life in the World Unseen*, 54.
7. Ibid.
8. Borgia, 66.
9. Borgia, *Here and Hereafter*, 82.
10. Borgia, *Life in the World Unseen*, 188.
11. Ibid., 190.
12. Borgia, *Life in the World Unseen*, 197.
13. Ibid., 199.
14. Ibid., 200.
15. Ibid.
16. Ibid.
17. Ibid.
18. Ritchie, *Return from Tomorrow*, 49.
19. Eadie, Betty J., *Embraced by the Light*, 40.
20. Burpo, Todd, *Heaven is for Real*, 111.
21. Ritchie, 49.

Wesley M. White

Chapter 10
Where Is the Spirit World?

> "They are not far from us, and know and understand our thoughts, feelings, and emotions, and are often pained therein."
> — *Joseph Smith*

Before we review additional accounts of those who have visited the spirit world, we need to recognize the challenge of finding words that describe an environment totally unfamiliar to us mortals.

As an example, a challenge faced when translating documents into Polynesian languages is the lack of the word for "snow." ("His countenance was like lightning, and his raiment white as snow" *Matthew 28:3*.) Those who have had NDEs face a similar challenge when attempting to describe an environment in which we have no more frame of reference than Polynesian islanders have of snow.

Dr. Kenneth Ring, co-founder of the Association for Near-Death Studies and author of the book *Heading Toward Omega*, writes, "There is absolutely no way in which ordinary human language can communicate the essence of ... NDEs."[1]

Given this difficulty, are there things we can learn about the next life? The answer is a resounding "Yes!"

A common question many ask about the spirit world is, *Where is it?* Many near death experiencers have come back with the impression it is on this earth, only invisible to the mortal eye.

President Brigham Young declared that the next abode is, "incorporated within this celestial system [even] on this earth."[2]

President Harold B. Lee taught that: "The spirit world is right here around us."[3]

Robert Hugh Benson wrote: "I did not realize the closeness of the two worlds."[4]

If the spirit world is close, the next question might be, *Are the inhabitants aware of us? Do they know of our activities, of our successes and failures?* It appears that in many situations the answer is yes. Many who have met deceased relatives during their brief visit to the next world have found that these relatives are aware of the lives of their loved ones on earth. They learn that they are not far from us and rejoice at our successes and are pained when we suffer.

Joseph Smith taught: "They are not far from us, and know and understand our thoughts, feelings, and emotions, and are often pained therein."[5]

President Brigham Young added: "They [the spirits in Paradise] can see us, but we cannot see them unless our eyes are opened." Spirit world inhabitants are generally much more aware of us mortals and our activities than we are of them.[6]

Robert Hugh Benson stated:

> The spirit world works constantly to make its power and force and presence felt by the whole earth world . . . but so little can be done, because the door is usually closed . . . Think of the evils that could be swept from the face of the earth!
>
> Humanity has, in effect, allowed the evil forces to dominate it . . . [The earth world] looks very dark to the godly in the spirit world] and [they] try very hard to bring a little light to it . . . Should they withdraw every element

of [their] influence, the earth would, in a very short time, be reduced to a state of complete and absolute barbarity and chaos.[7]

Perhaps some good and righteous people are taken prematurely (by our perceptions) to be an influence in the spirit world for good to this world, prone as it is toward barbarity and chaos.

My great-niece Camille recently recognized the closeness of the spirit world after enduring the horror and grief of losing her three-year-old son:

> We were a family of six. We had recently moved from California to Utah . . . It was Memorial Day and we had big plans to barbeque and roast hot dogs in the back yard and to swim in the community pool. It was 10:15 in the morning and I had just put our third child, three-year-old Wesley, down for a nap. Within an hour, I found myself barefoot in the emergency room of Primary Children's Hospital in Salt Lake City. I hadn't even noticed that I wasn't wearing shoes.
>
> Apparently, when I put Wesley down for a nap, a bolt from his toddler's bed had fallen out. Little Wesley found it, put it in his mouth, and he was choking on it.
>
> I expected that it would dislodge easily, but it wouldn't budge. An ambulance and helicopter ride later, my husband, Jeff, and I watched in horror as several nurses frantically performed chest compressions on our little tow-headed boy. His clothes were torn from EMTs attempts at CPR. Soon Jeff and I were looking into the sad eyes of the on-duty pediatric doctor. 'I'm so sorry,' she began, 'your son has experienced an unrecoverable accident.'
>
> She asked if we were ready to say good-bye. You're never ready to say good-bye. Shock had taken over. We were living one breath at a time, trying to navigate a horrible cloud of shock and grief. Wesley, my sweet enthusiastic little boy, had gone to heaven.
>
> The first few days after Wesley died, I felt him extremely close to me. Skeptics may say that it was just

wishful thinking or the need to be comforted by something, or the support I felt from friends and family who came running to our aid.

While the support of others was overwhelming in a positive way, the hole in my heart was still huge, gaping, wide open and raw. There was no 'what if 'or wishful thinking, or power on earth that could touch it nor fix it. The times I knew Wesley was nearby were unique, different than any comfort anyone or anything else could provide. I could feel him.

Everyone has a spirit. You could even call it a vibe: what you feel when you are around a specific person. It's their presence, a personality, a specific tangible identifiable feeling each person gives off. It's an energy and it's spiritual. Our loved ones who have passed on are close.[8]

In summary, the spirit world (the next life) is just around the bend. They (at least the righteous dead) are much more aware of us than we are of them, and they wish they could do more for us, but we are hard nuts to crack.

Rachel's Experience

Based on what I perceived during my NDE, I describe the spirit world as being incredibly near. I have witnessed the spirit world's close proximity to the mortal world and realized the separation of the two worlds is transparent. At times, I become overwhelmed with thoughts of how near the spirit world actually is to my temporal existence.

Firm belief and an absolute trust in an all-knowing Eternal Father confirms the significance of the interdependence between mortal life and the immortal. It is of utmost importance. Each is fully reliant on the other. The union is perfect, the connection eternal. I am reminded of the reality and feel of the nearness anew as I participate in temple work or attend funerals. At such times, my spirit recognizes the familiarity of heavenly loved ones coexisting on earth, even beside me. I feel of their warm presence in my heart and, quite literally, on my skin. I continue to feel a deep devotion and tenderness toward these many beloved acquaintances. I am conscious of their attachment to me and of their involvement in my daily life.

In the next chapter we will explore the possibility that some or all mortal experiences were planned and prepared for before we were born.

NOTES

1. Ring, Kenneth, *Heading Towards Omega*, 52. Ring has made a scientific study of 111 NDES from people around the world.
2. BYU Press, *Teachings of Presidents of the Church: Brigham Young*, Priesthood/Relief Society manual, 280.
3. BYU Press, *Teachings of Presidents of the Church: Harold B. Lee*, Priesthood/Relief Society manual, 58.
4. Borgia, Anthony, *Life in the World Unseen*, (dictated by Robert Hugh Benson), 186-197.
5. Smith, Joseph Fielding. *Teachings of the Prophet Joseph Smith*, 280.
6. Widtsoe, John A., *Discourses of Brigham Young*, 278.
7. Borgia, *Here and Hereafter*, 87.
8. Personal correspondence from Camille Packer McConnell to the author.

Wesley M. White

Chapter 11
Do We Have Guardian/Ministering Angels?

> "I promise you, dear children, that angels will minister unto you also. You may not see them, but they will be there to help you, and you will feel their presence."
>
> — *Ezra Taft Benson*

The Brethren clearly state that we believe in the ministering of angels, but the Church has not taken a doctrinal position concerning specific assignments of angels to those in this life (e.g., guardian angels). The terms "ministering angel" and "guardian angel" are used interchangeably.

The Prophet Joseph Smith referred to his guardian angel just two weeks before his martyrdom. Citing a recent dream, he said, "I was riding out in my carriage, and my guardian angel was along with me."[1]

Benjamin Johnson recounted a blessing he received from the Prophet, "He told the Lord I had been faithful to care for others, but I was worn out and sick, and that on my journey I would need His care, and he asked that a guardian angel might go with me from that day and stay with me through all my life."[2]

In the April 1989 General Conference, President Ezra Taft Benson declared: "I promise you, dear children, that angels will minister unto you also. You may not see them, but they will be there to help you, and you will feel their presence."[3]

With just over a year to live, Elder James E. Faust taught in an April 2006 General Conference: "We do not consciously realize the extent to which ministering angels affect our lives."[4]

In the same talk, he quoted President Joseph F. Smith:

> In like manner our fathers and mothers, brothers, sisters and friends who have passed away from this earth, having been faithful, and worthy to enjoy these rights and privileges, may have a mission given them to visit their relatives and friends upon the earth again, bringing from the divine Presence messages of love, of warning, or reproof and instruction, to those whom they have learned to love in the flesh. Many of us feel that we have had this experience. Their ministry has been and is an important part of the gospel.[5]

In General Conference of October 2008, Elder Jeffrey R. Holland gave a talk entitled "The Ministry of Angels." After speaking of Adam and Eve's expulsion from the Garden of Eden, he proclaimed:

> But God knew the challenge they would face, and He certainly knew how lonely and troubled they would sometimes feel. So He watched over his mortal family constantly, heard their prayers always, and sent prophets (and later apostles) to teach, counsel, and guide them. But in times of special need, He sent angels, divine messengers, to bless His children, reassure them that heaven was always very close and that His help was always very near.

Elder Holland went on to present several examples from the scriptures of the visitation of angels and then said:

> From the beginning down through the dispensations, God has used angels as His emissaries in conveying love and concern for His children. Usually, such beings are not seen, but seen or unseen they are always near. Sometimes their assignments are very grand and have significance for the whole world. Sometimes their messages are more private. Occasionally the angelic purpose

is to warn. But most often it is to comfort, to provide some form of merciful attention, guidance in difficult times.

Near the end of his discourse, Elder Holland testified:

> My beloved brothers and sisters, I testify that . . . always there are those angels who come and go all around us, seen and unseen, known and unknown, mortal and immortal.[6]

A year later, Elder Robert D. Hales (after explaining his recent time of great suffering and pain), said:

> As I studied the scriptures during this critical period of my life, the veil was thin and answers were given to me as they were recorded in lives of others who had gone through even more severe trials . . . I also learned that I would not be left alone to meet these trials and tribulations but that guardian angels would attend me. There were some that were near angels in the form of doctors, nurses, and most of all my sweet companion, Mary. And on occasion, when the Lord so desired, I was to be comforted with visitations of heavenly hosts that brought comfort and eternal reassurances in my time of need.[7]

Others who have studied the spirit world, or who have experienced an NDE, also testify of guardian angels. Robert Hugh Benson proclaimed: "Every soul that has ever been and is to be born upon the earth-plane has allocated to him—or her—a spirit guide."[8]

To those who do not believe in these constant guides, he warned, "That day will be whereon they meet in the spirit world their own guide, who probably knows more about their lives than they do themselves."[9]

Betty Eadie, in her bestselling book *Embraced by the Light*, expressed what most of us believe: "Each of us is receiving more help than we know."[10]

Our Personal Experience

Kay and I had almost identical experiences after our toddler was killed in an auto-pedestrian accident. Hers came just after she had picked up his broken body from the street and was rocking it in her arms before emergency personnel arrived. Mine came just after we returned home from the funeral.

In each case, we sensed keenly that we were surrounded by rejoicing spirits. The joy they emitted was greater than we had ever felt—a celebration beyond anything we had ever known—but our pain and grief at the time was so great that we were angry with them for reveling so joyously while our suffering was so great. However, over time, as the wounds from our loss have partially healed, we are comforted that our little two-year-old who had depended so greatly on us was excitedly received and cared for by others whom we suppose were deceased family members.

Angels Ministering Within the Spirit World

Now let's examine the angels who minister in the spirit world. Dr. Brent Top, Professor of Church History and Doctrine in the College of Religious Education at Brigham Young University, writes that assignments there include preparing clothing for those about to enter that realm and guiding newcomers, the latter one often performed by a family member or former friend.[11]

These ministering angels also serve as messengers to earth, perform missionary work, teach the gospel, and construct buildings in the spirit world.[12] The "housing boom" there, we can imagine, never ceases and is much accelerated in times of war and pestilence.

Just as temples in mortality have recorders, recording is a significant assignment in the spirit world. The scriptures often refer to what we call the Book of Life (there are twenty-three scriptural references to it in the Topical Guide). Many who have visited the spirit world speak of recorders who are assigned to keep accurate records of a person's life and then add those records to the Book of Life.[13]

A temple patron recently told me his eyes were opened while performing baptisms for the dead, and he saw a spiritual recorder writing the names and then saying them. The recorder pronounced some of the names differently than pronounced in the ordinance. If this is the case, what a comfort it is to us when we struggle with proxy name pronunciation in the temple.

Regarding temple work, an interesting reference to seeking out one's dead occurs in an article in the *Journal of Near-Death Studies*, in which Craig R. Lundahl, Ph.D., relates the following experience of one who had visited the Spirit World:

> It was between 10 and 11 o'clock that a visitor suddenly made his appearance in the room, and standing on the couch on which I lay, placed his hand on my head and asked if I was ready to go. I answered, 'Yes, and just at that instant I seemed to stand on the floor, my body lying on the bed. I looked around to see if my father could see us, but he seemed to be too interested in reading to have noticed us.
>
> We started off on our journey through space, seemingly with the rapidity of lightning. I asked my guide who he was. He answered he was one of the guardian angels sent to bring the dead. We soon reached a place where was congregated a great number of people—something similar to a market day in the old country. They seemed to have gathered for some purpose.
>
> I asked my guide what place this was, and he answered, 'That is the place where all your forefathers have gathered together and are waiting for two missionaries.' There seemed to be a stand erected close by for the missionaries to preach on. They came as it were directly; part of the congregation was noisy and inclined to be troublesome.

I asked my guide who these missionaries were, and he merely answered, 'The old man is the Apostle Matthias.' I understood by this that it was the Apostle Matthias who had filled the place of Judas Iscariot who betrayed the Savior, and the young man he further said, 'was an apostle from America who had lately been killed there'. . . then introduced me to the apostles by bowing his head which was returned by them. No hand shaking took place; the elder apostle said to me, 'Would you as soon go back, for it seems to fall to you to redeem your forefathers?' I answered, 'Yes.'[14]

Spirit World "Halls of Rest"

The last ministering angel assignment I address in this chapter requires some background. Before this study, I supposed that everything that mortal life does to "beat you up" remained in the grave. I have learned that there are some burdens so great that we even carry them over with us into the spirit world. Some afflictions have been so great, so prolonged, or so tragically sudden that they impact not only the body but also the mind, and there they remain after death as an impediment to progress.

Robert Hugh Benson explained:

> The earth world, in its blind ignorance, hurls hundreds of thousands of souls into this our land, but those who dwell in the higher realms are fully aware [of it] long before it happens . . . and a fiat goes forth to the realms nearer the earth to prepare for what is to come. These dire calamities of the earth-plane necessitate the building of more and more halls of rest.

He continues:

> In the great halls of rest there are expert nurses and doctors ready to treat those whose last earthly illness has been long and painful or whose passing into the spirit world has been sudden or violent.
>
> . . . These homes are a standing monument of shame to the earth world. The percentage is low, deplorably low,

of people who come into the spirit world with any knowledge at all of their new life and of the spirit world in general. All the countless souls without this knowledge have to be taken care of.[15]

Benson spoke of visiting two halls. The first was occupied by the spirits of those who had suffered lingering illness before dying:

> Immediately after their [deaths] they are sent gently into a deep sleep. In some cases, the sleep follows instantly—or practically without break— upon the physical death.
>
> Long illness prior to passing into the spirit world has a debilitating effect upon the mind, which in turn has its influence upon the spirit body. The latter is not serious, but the mind requires absolute rest of varying duration. Each case is treated individually, and eventually responds perfectly to the treatment.

He further said that the most difficult part of ministering to these souls is when they awaken:

> It has to be explained to the newly awakened soul that he has 'died' and is alive . . . When the true state of affairs has been gently and quietly explained to them, they often have an urgent desire to go back to earth, perhaps to those who are sorrowing, perhaps to those for whose care and welfare they were responsible. They are told that nothing can be done by their going back, and that others of experience will take care of those circumstances that are so distressing them.

Benson also visited a large hall of those whose passing had been sudden and violent. These received special care. They were immediately placed into a state of rest. When they awoke, "the suddenness of their departure added far greater confusion to the mind...." He reports that their passing had been so sudden that there seemed to be no break between life and death. Such people, he said, are taken in hand quickly by bands of spirits who devote all their time and the whole of their energies to such work.[16]

Benson lauds "these gentle, patient helpers wrestling mentally—and sometimes almost physically—with people who are ignorant of the fact they are dead." He notes that visitors from higher realms make frequent visits to these halls. The love of God, often manifested by His representatives, permeates the next life.[17]

Rachel's Experience

There were many times during my recovery that were very upsetting, frustrating, and discouraging. Looking back, I am amazed at the degree of pain and fear I endured. I attribute this miraculous ability not as my own but to the Savior and His remarkable power to provide mercy and grace. I truly lived without physical distress, mental anguish, or emotional sorrow during this time. I had the 'privilege of soaring among immortal beings and of enjoying to a certain extent, the presence of God.'

I was aware of countless immortal beings, of past and future generations, and knew of their love and tenderness they had for me. Gram was not my only guardian angel but rather one of many who spiritually and physically supported and protected me throughout this great trial. This blessing continued for several weeks, if not months. These unseen angels still bring much needed peace to my spirit even today. I feel of their concern daily. Though the veil is no longer transparent to me, and despite the difficulty of seeing my guardian angels physically, I know of their presence and feel of their love . . . .

Summary

Whether or not we are each assigned a particular guardian angel has yet to be revealed. But it is clear that select spirits from the next world minister to those in this life, as well as to those with special needs in the next. We are never outside of God's loving plan for the progress of his children.

NOTES

1. Crowther, Duane S., *Life Everlasting: A Definitive Study of Life After Death*, 262.
2. Ibid.
3. Benson, Ezra Taft, "To the Children of the Church," General Conference, April 1989.
4. Faust, James E., "A Royal Priesthood," General Conference, April 2006.
5. Ibid.
6. Holland, Jeffrey R., "Ministry of Angels," General Conference, October 2008.
7. Hales, Robert D., "The Covenant of Baptism," General Conference, October 2010.
8. Borgia, Anthony, *Life in the World Unseen*, (dictated by Robert Hugh Benson)183.
9. Ibid. 185.
10. Eadie, Betty J., *Embraced by the Light*, 53.
11. Top, Brent L. and Wendy C., *Glimpses Beyond Death's Door*, 156-157
12. Crowther, 191.
13. Ibid., 191.
14. Lundahl, Craig R., "Angels in Near Death Experiences," *Journal of Near-Death Studies*, 11(1), Fall 1992, 53.
15. Borgia, 73.
16. Ibid., 115.
17. Ibid., 75.

Wesley M. White

Chapter 12
Temples in the Spirit World

> "Upon the summit . . . a Temple stood, whose vast dome, massive pillars and solid walls were of unsullied pearl, and through whose great mullioned windows shone a white radiance that swallowed up the golden glow of the twilight and made it its own."
> — *Rebecca Ruter Springer*

The word temple has different meanings among different peoples: we call some edifices in the ruins of Central and South America temples; the ancient Greeks had the Temple of Hephaestus in Athens; Borobudur is a large Indonesian Buddhist temple; Angkor Wat in Cambodia is the largest Hindu temple in the world, so, when considering whether temples play a role in the spirit world, the short answer would be that it depends on how you define "temple." But to most, a temple is a sacred edifice where one can draw closer to deity.

One of Webster's definitions of a temple is "a building for Mormon sacred ordinances."

Wilford Woodruff, while serving as President of the Church, spoke of seeing Joseph Smith in the spirit world: "In the night vision I saw him at the door of the temple in heaven."[1]

Rebecca Ruter Springer, in her Civil War-era book, *My Dream of Heaven*, wrote of seeing a temple in her NDE: "Upon the summit . . . a Temple stood, whose vast dome, massive pillars and solid walls were of unsullied pearl, and through whose great mullioned windows shone a white radiance that swallowed up the golden glow of the twilight and made it its own."[2]

I suppose that only the higher realms afford a temple and that the functions of the temple vary from realm to realm according to what the inhabitants are prepared to receive.

Robert Hugh Benson provided more specifics:

> There were fine broad thoroughfares of emerald green lawns in perfect cultivation, radiating like the spokes of a wheel, from a central building which, as we could see was the hub of the whole city.
>
> There was a great shaft of pure light descending upon the dome of this building, and we felt instinctively—without Edwin [the guide] having to tell us—that in this temple we could gather to send up our thanks to the Great Source of all, and that there we should find none other than the Glory of God in Truth.[3]

Benson continued:

> Above us was a great dome of exquisitely wrought gold, which reflected the hundreds of colors that shone from the rest of the building.[4]
>
> We spirit people are conscious of the eternal thanks that we owe to the Great Father for giving us such unbound happiness in a land where so many upon earth deny the reality.[5]

He provides touching details of the meeting he attended:

> The sanctuary, which was of spacious dimensions, was filled with many beings from higher realms, with the exception of a space in the center, which I guessed was reserved for our visit. We were all of us seated, and we conversed quietly among ourselves. Presently, we were aware of the presence of a stately figure of a man with jet-black hair, who was closely followed—very much to my surprise—by the kindly Egyptian that we had met at Edwin's house on the realm boundary.

To those who would already witness such visitations, their arrival was at once the indication of the coming of a high personage, and we all accordingly rose to our feet. Then, before our eyes, there appeared a first light, which might almost be described as dazzling, but as we concentrated our eyes upon it, we immediately became attuned to it, and we felt no sensation of spiritual discomfort... It was toned down to accord with ourselves and our realm ... And in the center there slowly took shape the form of a visitant.

As it gained in density, we could see that he was a man whose appearance was that of youth—spiritual youth...

His movements were majestic and as he raised his arms, he set forth a blessing upon us all. We remained standing and silent while our thoughts ascended to Him Who sent such a glorious being....

It is not possible for me to convey to you one fraction of the exultation of the spirit that I felt while in his presence, though distant, of this heavenly guest. But I do know that not for long could I have remained in that temple while he was there without a crushing consciousness that I was low, very, very low upon the scale of spiritual evolution and progression and yet I knew that he was sending out to me, as to us all, thoughts of encouragement, of good hope, of kindness in the very highest degree, that made me feel that I must never, never despair of attaining to the highest spiritual realm, and there was good and useful work ready for me to do in the service of man, and that in doing thereof I would have the whole of the spiritual realm behind me—it seems they are behind every single soul who works in the service of man.[6]

It seems that a common purpose of all spirit world temples is to: 1) provide a special place in which to worship and express thanks to God, 2) feel of His great love for all His children, and 3) receive encouragement to progress toward becoming as He is.

Rachel's Experience

Understandably, many fear the transition of mortal to immortal existence. It is human nature to feel anxious about the unknown. Based on my NDE, I am comforted by the memory of life beyond the grave. I feel tremendously blessed to have discovered the unconditional love of my deceased ancestors and enjoy knowing of their nearness. Serving in the temple has also dispelled my fear of the next life. I rely on their support greatly, particularly in times of tribulation or uncertainty. I find much relief as I call upon them for direction and reassurance in doing the Lord's will.

When my earthly time is complete and it is time to enter the spirit world, I know I will not fear. Although my mortal mind no longer recalls the intricacy of the next life nor understands the vastness of eternity, I know my spirit did. I may feel uncertain up until the precise time of transition, yet I have faith I will remember and comprehend with exactness the details of eternal life, as I have before. I will at last be able to see the faces of my beloved heavenly friends and relatives, and any fear will be replaced with complete peace.

NOTES

1. Crowther, Duane S., *Life Everlasting: A Definitive Study of Life After Death*, 164.
2. Ibid., 234.
3. Springer, Rebecca Ruter, *My Dream of Heaven*, 100. This book was recently republished, although the events related therein occurred shortly after the American Civil War (1861–65). I include this book because the author, not a member of the Church, references eternal marriage as a part of her NDE.
4. Ibid.
5. Ibid.
6. Ibid.

Chapter 13
Missionary Work in the Spirit World

> "It appears that people who die without the gospel do not necessarily hear it preached as soon as they enter the spirit world, but only as they are ready."
> — *Brent and Wendy Top*

As a church, we have a strong commitment to missionary work no matter where we find ourselves—even after we leave mortality. Let us look at some of the differences from here to there.

One difference is magnitude. Wikipedia estimates that one hundred billion people have lived on the earth thus far.[1] Joseph F. Smith saw in vision that the gospel must be preached to all (see *D&C 138:30*). To illustrate the magnitude of this task, it equates roughly to 40,000 spirit world inhabitants for every member of the Church living today.

Of the methodology in the spirit world, Emanuel Swedenborg (1688-1772) taught that "each and every individual can be taught as befits his own intrinsic character and his ability to receive." He offered the example of:

> . . . people devoted to the Mohammed religion who lived a moral life in the world, recognizing one Divine Being . . . [after being taught in the spirit world] and recognizing the Lord as the Essential Prophet . . .

> [they] withdraw from Mohammad, because he cannot help them, they approach the Lord, worship Him, and recognize what is Divine about Him. Then they are taught in the Christian religion . . . Mohammedans are taught by angels who were once involved in that religion and have turned to Christianity; the heathen too are taught by their own angels.[2]

From their research, Brother Brent Top and his wife Wendy (authors of *Glimpses Beyond Death's Door*) find missionary work to be less proactive in the next life. "It appears that people who die without the gospel do not necessarily hear it preached as soon as they enter the spirit world, but only as they are ready."[3]

Robert Hugh Benson explained it this way:

> It must not be thought that we were part of a campaign to convert people, in the religious sense in which the word is used on earth. Far from it. We do not interfere with people's beliefs nor their viewpoints; we only give our services when they are asked for in such matters, or when we see that by giving them, we can affect some useful purpose. Neither do we spend our time walking about evangelizing people, but when the call comes for help then we answer it instantly. But there comes a time when spiritual unrest will make itself felt, and that is the turning point in the life of many a soul who has been confined and restricted by wrong views, whether religious or otherwise. Religion is not responsible for all mistaken ideas![4]

Two aspects of Benson's explanation gladden my heart. First, it sounds as if there is no tracting in the spirit world, and second, our deeply held misconceptions, even across a very broad range, will eventually be brought perfectly into line with Truth.

It may be that missionary work is more proactive in this mortal life, because: 1) we are bound by the constraints of time; 2) we are preparing for the pending Second Coming and the Lord has informed us that the hour is near at hand; and 3) because the world's moral compass is wavering and permissiveness is rampant, preparing for the Second Coming must accelerate as opposition and wickedness increase.

NOTES

1. Wikipedia, "The World's Population."
2. Top, Brent L. and Wendy C., *Glimpses Beyond Death's Door*, 144.
3. Ibid., 145.
4. Borgia, Anthony, *Life in the World Unseen*, 77, 128.

Wesley M. White

Chapter 14
Time, Space, Expeditions, and Discoveries in the Spirit World

> "My visit to the spirit world seemed brief, only a matter of seconds, yet it seems impossible to have communicated with so many and obtained such a high and clear level of understanding in such a short amount of time. Time in the spirit world is different from time in mortality."
> — Rachel Andersen

Man may dream of time travel and write novels about it, but we are still bound in rigid time. We may wish to grow up more quickly when we are young and wish the years would pass more slowly as we age, but Time moves unescapably, at a constant pace, beyond our control.

In the next life, we will step onto new ground. Elder Maxwell wrote, "We cannot fully understand time while we are inside of it."[1]

Relatively few of God's children have been allowed to "step out" of time while in mortality, and we must depend heavily on their personal accounts. Moses "beheld the world upon which he was created; and Moses beheld the world and the end thereof, and all the children of men which are, and which were created." (*Moses 1:8*)

The brother of Jared from the Book of Mormon had a similar experience: "[God] showed unto the brother of Jared all the inhabitants of the earth which had been, and also all that would be, and he withheld them not from his sight, even unto the ends of the world." (*Ether 3:25*)

Obviously, Moses and the brother of Jared stepped out of the constraints of time as we know them.

Those who have experienced what time felt like in the spirit world during their NDEs, of course, find it difficult to explain it to the rest of us. After his NDE, Dr. Eben Alexander wrote, "Time in this place was different from the simple linear time we experience on earth and is as hopelessly difficult to describe as every other aspect of it."[2] When asked how long she had been in the spirit world, another NDEer replied, "It could have been a minute, or 10,000 years."[3]

Others expressed time in the spirit world as "changed, compounded, absent,"[4] or "compressed."[5] It is much less constraining than mortal time. Emanuel Swedenborg stated, "time and space no longer pose the obstacles they do in physical life."[6]

As an example, Dr. George Ritchie said of his NDE, "It would have taken weeks of ordinary time even to glance at so many events, yet I had no sense of minutes passing."[7] Ritchie "died" in a military hospital where careful records were kept. The log shows he was dead for only nine minutes.[8]

The Prophet Joseph Smith spoke of the angels who dwell among the Gods: "All things for their glory are manifest, past, present, and future, and are continually before the Lord." (*D&C 130:7*)

C. S. Lewis expressed it this way:

> But suppose God is outside and above the timeline. In that case, what we call 'tomorrow' is visible to Him in just the same way as what we call 'today.' All the days are now for Him. He does not remember you doing things yesterday; He simply sees you doing them, because, though you have lost yesterday, He has not.

> He does not 'foresee' you doing things tomorrow; He simply sees you doing them; because, though tomorrow is not yet there for you, it is for Him.[9]

While serving as proxies for the dead in temples, we often state, "He (or she) has waited a long time for this ordinance." The less-constraining nature of time in the spirit world renders this conclusion overly simplistic. It would be more accurate to say, "It has been many earth years since he (or she) lived," because he or she now lives outside of "time" as we experience it.

Robert Hugh Benson made a valiant effort to explain time in the spirit world. He tried to give us the best understanding possible while we are yet confined to the "time" of mortality:

> It is commonly thought by people of the earth-plane that in the spirit world time and space do not exist. That is wrong. [There is] both, but [the] conception of them differs from that of the earth world . . . [There are] no clocks . . . no recurrent seasons, no alterations of light and darkness or external indicators of time, and, in addition, no personal reminder, common to the incarnate, of hunger, thirst, and fatigue, or aging . . . When [those in the next life] look forward to the arrival of a relative or friend into the spirit world it is towards the event we cast our minds, not the year in which the event is to take place.[10]

Rachel's Experience

> I often recall my experience with the afterlife as a single event—visiting with Gram—but I also communicated with others, including my maternal grandfather and my future children. This causes me to wonder if such communications were at separate times.
>
> My visit to the spirit world seemed brief, only a matter of seconds, yet it seems impossible to have communicated with so many and obtained such a high and clear level of understanding in such a short amount of time. Time in the spirit world is different from time in mortality.

The Prophet Joseph Smith may have explained spirit world time the best when he suggested that if we could gaze into heaven for five minutes, we would know more about the topic than if we studied it all our lives.

My visit to the spirit world could not have been longer that ten (earthly) days, but the vastness of information and understanding gained in that short time far exceeds mortal comprehension.

Space

Robert Hugh Benson taught:

> Space must exist in the spirit world . . . [for]example: Standing at the window of [an] upper room of [a] house, I can see across huge distances whereon are many houses and grand buildings. In the distance I can see the city with many more great buildings. Dispensed throughout the whole wide prospect are woods and meadows, rivers and streams, just as these occupy space in the earth world.[11]

Travel

You may remember Elder Maxwell listed vastness as one of the four primary characteristics of the spirit world. However, that vastness does not burden realm inhabitants with the rigors we associate with travel. The best way to understand this vastness and the mode of travel in one of the higher realms is to take a tour with Robert Hugh Benson—a tour he initially didn't want to take.

Explained Benson:

> I know I can travel uninterruptedly through enormous areas of space, areas far greater than the whole of the earth area trebled in size, or greater. I have not yet transversed anything like one fraction of the full extent of my realm, but I am free to do so.[12]

Benson provided us a hypothetical example:

> We decide to walk through the gardens and woods. The house is some 'distance' away, but that does not mat-

ter, because we never suffer from 'physical' fatigue, and we are not otherwise engaged. We walk along together, talking happily, and after a certain lapse of 'time' we arrive at the house of our friend, and we have covered the intervening space on foot. However, we choose to rapidly make the journey from [the] house to the [city]. We overcome the substantial distance in a moment, dispensing with time for the occasion.[13]

The Academia of the City

Robert Hugh Benson offers us a different picture of city life than we see on earth. Soon after Benson's arrival in the spirit world, his guide offered him a tour of a nearby city. Benson was not anxious to go. He said:

> My mind had reverted to the narrow streets and crowded pavements of the earth; the buildings huddled together because space is so valuable and costly; the heavy, tainted air, made worse by streams of traffic; I had thought of hurry and turmoil, and all the restlessness of commercial life and the excitement of passing pleasure.[14]

What a pleasant surprise awaited him. He wrote:

> I had no conception of a city of eternal beauty, as far removed from an earthly city as the light of day is from black night. Here were the broad thoroughfares of emerald green lawns in perfect cultivation . . . .

It is obvious Benson was not visiting one of the lower realms. Benson continued to explain this particular city's purpose:

> The city was devoted to the pursuit of learning, to the study and practice of the arts, and to the pleasures of all in this realm. It was exclusive to none, but free for all to enjoy with equal right. Here it was possible to carry on so many of those pleasant fruitful occupations which had been denied them, for a variety of reasons, perhaps such as living during the Dark Ages whilst they were incarnate. There was not a single dark location in the city. The light radiating from God filled every corner and crevasse.[15]

The view of the city is unobstructed by tall buildings. There is no need for skyscrapers because spirit world space is unlimited and travel is simple.

While in the city, they visited a large hall dedicated to the art of painting:

> This hall was of great size and had a long gallery, on the walls of which were hanging every great masterpiece known to man. They were arranged in such a way that every step of earthly progression could be followed in proper order, beginning with the earliest times, and continuing down to the present day.
>
> Every style of painting was represented, gathered from all parts of the earth. It must not be thought such a collection, as we were now viewing, is only of interest and service to people who have a full appreciation and understanding of the painter's art. Such could not be further from the case.[16]

He continued:

> There were groups listening to the words of able teachers, who were demonstrating the various phases in the history of art as exemplified upon the walls, and they were, at the same time, giving such a clear and interesting position none could fail to understand.[17]

Concerning the quality of the artwork, Benson wrote the following:

> Several of the pictures I recognized as I had seen their "originals" in the earth's galleries. Ruth (a recently deceased woman also under the tutelage of Edwin) and I were astonished when Edwin told us what we had seen in those galleries were not the originals at all.
>
> We were now seeing the originals for the first time. What we had seen was an earthly counterpart, which was perishable from the usual causes—for example, from fire or the general disintegration through the passage of time. But here we were viewing the direct results of the thoughts of the painter, created in the etheric before he transferred those thoughts to his earthly canvas.

It could be plainly observed, in many cases, where the earthly picture fell short of that which the painter had in his mind. He had endeavored to reproduce the exact conception, but through physical limitations this exact concept had eluded him.

In some instances, it had been the pigments that had been to fault when, in the early times, the artist had been unable to procure or evolve the shade of color he wanted.

But though he lacked physically, his mind had known precisely what he wished to do. He had built it up in the spirit—the results of which we were now able to see—while he had failed to do so on the material canvas.[18]

Animation

Benson said it was impossible to convey to mortals the paramount difference in this spirit world artwork. "These pictures were alive.... They were never flat.... The subject stood out as though it were a model.... The colors glowed with life, even among the very early works."[19]

This leads to an important aspect of "Life," certainly in the higher realms and perhaps even the middle realms: universal animation. Everything is "living," or in other words, contains life.

Benson clarified that nothing there is inert.[20] For example, gems shine from within, rather than reflecting light.[21] This animation comes from what Benson calls "The Source." He provides an example:

A recently deceased young man is interested in horticulture, particularly flowers. He tries his hand at spirit world flower creation. He must learn much to organize a beautiful flower, but when he succeeds, the flower must be animated. A request is sent to the highest realms, and 'spirit' is instilled into the flower. From that time, it possesses life and radiates beauty, fragrance, and the joyous praising of God.[22]

This animation is probably what the scriptures refer to as the Light of Christ.

As Benson illustrated, in at least the higher realms of the spirit world, everything is "alive," or animated, but many things do not have what he referred to as "will." The flower provides an excellent example. It is filled with joy and love for God and receives joy by sharing its beauty and fragrance, but it is perfectly content to be a flower. It has no desire to be anything else or anywhere else.

And Benson captured the delights of spirit world water when he related that one can slip beneath its surface and enjoy its warm embrace as it folds its living arms around you. It soothes, it invigorates, it inspires. It will produce the most beautiful sounds when it is disturbed on its surface.[23]

Because water is so essential to our lives and carries such great symbolism in the gospel, I include Rebecca Ruter Springer's similar experiences noted in *My Dream of Heaven*. We begin in the middle of a conversation with her brother, who had brought her from mortality to the spirit world. She was severely ill, and he desired to provide her with a brief spiritual rest.

> 'Ah!' said my brother in a tone of self-reproach.' I am inconsiderate.' And lifting me gently to my feet said, 'Come, I want to show you the river.'
>
> When we reached the brink of the river, but a few steps distance, I found the lovely sward ran even to the water's edge, and in some places, I found flowers blooming placidly down in the depths, among the many-colored pebbles with which the entire bed of the river was lying.
>
> 'I want you to see these beautiful stones,' said my brother, stepping into the water and urging me to do the same.
>
> I drew back timidly, saying, 'I fear it is cold.'
>
> 'Not in the least,' he said, with a reassuring smile.
>
> 'Just as I am?' I said, glancing down at my lovely robe, which to my great joy, I found was similar to those

of the dwellers in that happy place.

'Just as you are,' with another reassuring smile.

Thus encouraged, I too, stepped into the gently flowing river, and to my great surprise found the water, in both temperature and density, almost identical with the air.

Deeper and deeper grew the stream as we passed on, until I felt the soft, sweet ripples playing about my throat. As I stopped, my brother said, 'A little further still.'

'It will go over my head,' I postulated.

'Well, and what then?'

'I cannot breathe under that water—I will suffocate.'

An amused twinkle came into his eyes, though he said soberly enough, 'We do not do those things here.' I realized the absurdity in my position, and with a happy laugh said, 'All right; come on,' and plunged headlong into the bright water, which soon bubbled and rippled several feet above my head.

To my surprise and delight, I found I could not only breathe, but laugh and talk, see and hear, as naturally underwater as above it. I sat down amid the many-colored pebbles, and filled my hands with them, as a child would have done.

My brother lay down upon them, as he would have done on the green sward, and laughed and talked joyously with me . . . and the sensation was delightful. I threw back my loose hair and rubbed my arms and then my throat and again thrust my fingers through my long loose hair, thinking at the time what a tangled [mess] it would be when I left the water.

Then the thought came, as we rose to return. 'What are we to do for towels?' For the earth thought still clung to me; and I wondered too, if the lovely robe was not entirely to behold.

As we neared the shore and my head once more emerged from the water, my flesh, my hair, and even my beautiful garments, were soft and dried . . . The material out of which my robe was fashioned was unlike anything I'd ever seen. It was soft and light and shown with a faint luster, reminding me more of silk crêpe than anything I could recall, only infinitely more beautiful. It fell about me in soft, graceful folds, which the water seemed to have rendered even more lustrous than before.

'What marvelous water! What wonderful air!' I said to my brother, as we again stepped up on the flowery sward. 'Are all rivers here like this one?'

'Not just the same but similar,' he replied. We walked on a few steps and then I turned and looked back at the shining river flowing on tranquilly. 'Frank, what has the water done for me?' I said, 'I feel as though I could fly.'

He looked at me with earnest tender eyes as he answered gently, 'It has washed away the last of the earth life and fitted you for the new life which you have entered.' 'It is divine!' I whispered. 'Yes, it is divine,' he replied.[24]

There is no ordinance we know of that is associated with entry into the "divine" waters of the spirit world. However, apparently, stains and cares are washed away by immersion in it, and souls are reinvigorated. By mortal baptism, our earthly sins—through priesthood power—are washed away, and we are exhilarated.

This is certainly not gospel doctrine, but rather just recognition of a similitude.

The Physical Brain and the Eternal Mind

As you probably expect, NDEers routinely report that learning in the spirit world is exponentially easier and faster than on earth, and that you forget nothing. (I can't fathom an existence where I'm not constantly searching for my wallet and car keys.) And it gets even better; you will have all the knowledge you attained in mortality that "escaped" your mortal brain.

Although your physical brain has forgotten many things, your mind has not. Every event of your life and all that you have learned and experienced lives on in the mind and is available again once it is unencumbered by the brain.[25]

World History

Together, Robert Hugh Benson, Ruth, and Edwin later visited the hall of literature, with equally astounding results:

> Edwin led us into one spacious apartment which contained the histories of all the nations upon the earth-plane. To anyone who has a knowledge of earthly history, the volumes with which the shelves of this section of the great library were filled, would prove illuminating. The reader would be able to gain, for the first time, the truth about the history of his country. Every word contained in these books was the literal truth. Concealment is impossible because nothing but the truth can enter these realms.[27]
>
> I have since returned to the library and spent much profitable time among its countless books. I have dipped into history, and I was amazed when I started to read. I naturally expected to find history would be treated in the manner with which we are all familiar, but with the essential difference that now I should be presented with the truth of all historical acts and events.
>
> The latter I soon discovered was the case, but I made another discovery that for the first moment left me astounded. I found that with the statements of pure fact of every act of persons of historical note, by statesmen in whose hands was the government of their countries, by kings who were at the head of those same countries, side by side with such statements was the blunt naked truth of each motive governing or underlying their numerous acts—the truth beyond disputation. Many of such motives were elevated; many, many of them were utterly base; many were misconstrued, many distorted.
>
> Written indelibly upon these spirit annals were the true narratives of thousands upon thousands of human beings, who, whilst upon their earthly journey, had been active participants in the affairs of their country. Some were victims to others' treachery and baseness; some were the cause or origin of that treachery and baseness. None was spared, none was omitted. It was all there for all to see—the truth, with nothing extenuated, nothing suppressed.

He added:

> Although these books witness against the perpetrators of so many dark deeds in the world's history, they also bore witness to many deeds both great and noble.[28]

Concluding the visit to the history library, Benson stated:

> I also delved into [Christian] church history, and the revelations I received in that direction were no better than those in the political sphere. They were, in fact, worse, considering in whose name so many diabolical deeds were committed by men who, outwardly professing to serve God, were but instruments of men as base as themselves.[29]

Technology

Concerning spirit world technology, Benson said, "All of the major discoveries that are of service to the earth-plane have come and will always come, from the spirit world." He explained, "a mere hint to an earthly scientist is enough to set him upon the track of a dozen or more other discoveries. All that the scientists here are concerned with is the initial discovery, and in most cases the rest will follow."[30]

None of the students or researchers sought attention or recognition. They would not inhabit such higher realms if they had such motives.

Ritchie wrote, "I understood that their work was motivated by sincere interest in what they were learning and a desire to help make the universe a better place to live, not money or fame."[31]

The next-life observations of the arts and humanities detailed in this book primarily come from Benson. That would be expected. Benson wrote more than 30 books and plays, most concerning theology. I have read some of them.

On the other hand, Ritchie had majored in chemistry, with minors in physics and calculus. He was also the first person to write a bestseller about a personal NDE (*Return from Tomorrow*). He added a doctorate in psychiatry after his NDE. It is natural that his primary interest while visiting the next life would be in the sciences.

Research

Ritchie marveled as soon as he arrived at the realm's research facility. He said that the facility was, "bigger than all the buildings in downtown Washington, DC, put together."[32]

He visited a building that was "covered with technological machinery." The scientists/engineers were continuing in the same area of study they pursued in mortality, striving for the goal of improving the universe. They "were using instruments I had never seen and could not begin to understand. Not only could I not understand their instruments, I cannot begin to comprehend their advanced technical thinking."

He added, "They were so advanced in so many ways that it would be like taking my son, when he was six years of age, to one of the research laboratories at the University of Virginia and expecting him to comprehend what he was seeing."[33]

Like Moses (*Moses 3:5*), Ritchie declared all things were created spiritually before their physical existence upon the earth. He wrote:

> Why is it that the inventors in different parts of the earth produce the same ideas at about the same time—Ford in America, Bentley in England, Peugeot in France? I believe I was shown the place where those who've already gone before us are doing research and want to help us when we begin to seriously turn deep within for answers.[34]
>
> I prided myself a little on the beginning of a scientific education . . . But if these were scientific activities of some kind, they were so far beyond anything I knew that I couldn't even guess what field they were in . . . Some

vast experiment was being pursued, perhaps dozens and dozens of such experiments.[35]

Interestingly, Ritchie saw some of his NDE come to fruition on earth. Almost a decade later, he was thumbing through the pages of *Life* magazine. The Atomic Energy Commission had allowed *Life*'s artists to draw portions of the second U.S. atomic submarine engine. Ritchie commented: "I . . . felt so certain I'd seen the whole operation." The magazine reported that engineers would build the engine inside a huge sphere-shaped building. Ritchie continued:

> The thing I had seen was finished and operating . . . then I remembered [where I had seen it]. It was in that campus-like realm inhabited by beings wrapped in thought . . . that I had stood in in 1943, as the earth measures time, staring at this [same] huge sphere-shaped building, [even] walking through its intricate fittings.[36]

As this chapter illustrates, our Earth receives much help and inspiration from the spirit world. However, it is much less than we could receive if we lived on a higher spiritual plane. Benson declared, "there will surely come a time when the truth will be diffused throughout the earth."[37] Though Benson doesn't elucidate, I suppose that that time will be during the Millennium, which is the thousand-year period after the Second Coming of the Savior.

What a magnificent day it will be when this world and the spirit world finally function in total harmony!

NOTES

1. Maxwell, Neal A., *The Promise of Discipleship*, 83.
2. Alexander, Eben, *Proof of Heaven*, 67.
3. Moody, Raymond, *Reflections on Life after Death*, 215.
4. Top, Brent L. and Wendy C., *Glimpses Beyond Death's Door*, 127.
5. Moody, *The Light Beyond*, 17.
6. Top, 121.

7. Ritchie, George G., *Return from Tomorrow*, 51.
8. Ibid., 79.
9. Lewis, C. S., *Mere Christianity*, 135.
10. Borgia, Anthony, *Life in the World Unseen*, 120-4.
11. Ibid., 124.
12. Ibid.
13. Ibid.
14. Ibid., 44.
15. Ibid.
16. Ibid.
17. Ibid., 44-5.
18. Ibid.
19. Borgia, *More Life in the World Unknown*, 65.
20. Ibid., 149.
21. Ibid., 107.
22. Ibid., 28-9.
23. Ibid., 46.
24. Springer, Rebecca Ruter, *My Dream of Heaven*, 8–11
25. Borgia, *Life in the World Unseen*, 49.
26. Ibid. 49.
27. Ibid., 48.
28. Ibid., 60.
29. Ibid.
30. Ritchie, *Ordered to Return*, 44.
31. Ibid., 43.
32. Ibid., 44.
33. Ibid., 43.
34. Ibid., 69-70.
35. Ritchie, *Return from Tomorrow*, 120.
36. Borgia, 187.
37. Ibid.

Wesley M. White

Chapter 15
Color and Music in the Spirit World

> "Light in the spirit world doesn't necessarily reflect off anything. It comes from within and appears to be a living essence. A million, a billion colors are possible."
> — *Betty J. Eadie*

Color

As one might expect, spirit world color is greatly amplified and purified, and has a broader spectrum. In her book, *Embraced by the Light,* Betty J. Eadie described her visit to a garden:

> I walked on the grass for a time. It was crisp, cool, and brilliant green, and it felt alive under my feet. But what filled me with awe in the garden more than anything were the intense colors. We have nothing like them. When light strikes an object here, the light reflects off that object in a certain color. Thousands of shades are possible. Light in the spirit world doesn't necessarily reflect off anything. It comes from within and appears to be a living essence. A million, a billion colors are possible.[1]

Music

Many who have experienced the next life remark on the indescribably beautiful music there.[2] In Anthony Borgia's book,

Robert Hugh Benson stated that music is a vital element of the spirit world and that it greatly enhances one's joy. He added:

> The whole attitude toward music held by so many people on the earth undergoes a great change when they eventually come to [the] spirit [world]. Music is looked upon by many on the earth-plane as merely a pleasant diversion, a pleasant adjunct to the earthly life, but by no means a necessity.
>
> Here it is part of life . . . it is part of natural existence, as are flowers and trees, grass and water, and hills and dales. It is an element of our spiritual nature.[3]

The Special Relationship Between Music and Color

Not only are music and colors greatly improved from our "dreary" plane, but Benson proclaims that in the spirit world they are one and the same. He states, "Color and sound—that is, musical sound—are interchangeable terms. In the higher spirit world realms, to perform some act that will produce color is also to produce a musical sound."[4]

Earlier in his spirit-world experience, Benson noted this intra-relationship of color and music portrayed in the flowers and the water:

> There was another astonishing feature I noticed when I drew near to them, and that was the sound of music that enveloped them, making such soft harmonies as corresponded exactly and perfectly with the gorgeous colors of the flowers themselves . . . The water that sparkles and flashes colors is also creating musical sounds of purity and beauty . . . The sounds are in perfect accord with the colors . . . and the perfect combination of both sight and sound is perfect harmony.[5]

Dr. Eben Alexander substantiated, "Seeing and hearing were not separate." He could hear the visual beauty of flowers, bodies of water, scenery, and even people.[6]

The Concert

An illustration of the color–music relationship comes from Benson's description of a concert that he attended in the spirit world:

> The opening movement was of a subdued nature as regards its volume and sound, and we noticed that the instant the music commenced, a bright light seemed to rise up from the direction of the orchestra until it floated, in a flat surface, level with the topmost seats, where it remained as an iridescent cover to the whole amphitheater.
>
> As the music proceeded, this broad sheet of light grew in strength and density, forming as it were, a firm foundation for what was to follow . . . .
>
> Presently, at equal spaces round the circumference of the theater, four towers of light shot up into the sky in long tapering pinnacles of luminosity . . . .
>
> In the meanwhile, the central area of light had thickened still more, and was beginning to rise slowly in the shape of an immense dome covering the whole theater . . . the most delicate colors were diffused throughout the whole of the etheric structure . . . .
>
> The music was still being played, and in response to it, the whole coloring of the dome changed, first to one shade, then to another, and many times a delicate blend of a number of shades according to the variation in theme or movement of the music . . . It is difficult to give any adequate idea of the beauty of this wonderful musical structure . . . .
>
> Unlike the earth where music can only be heard, there we had both heard and seen it.[7]

Music and color, working together in harmony, will be a beautiful, enriching, inspiring new aspect of life, with the garish and trashy aspects of both soon forgotten.

NOTES

1. Eadie, Betty J., *Embraced by the Light*, 78-79.
2. Moody, Raymond, *Life After Life*, 46.

3. Borgia , Anthony, *Life in the World Unseen*, 46.
4. Ibid, 63.
5. Ibid., 63-64.
6. Alexander, Eben, *Proof of Heaven*, 75.
7. Borgia, 67-68.

Chapter 16
Sociality in the Spirit World

> "When the surf of the centuries has made the great pyramids so much sand, the everlasting family will still be standing, because it is a celestial institution...."
> — Neal A. Maxwell

When we eventually transition to the spirit world, we will be starkly aware of how our sociality in mortality had far-reaching effects on our next life. Author Betty J. Eadie recorded:

> I saw the disappointment that I had caused others, and I cringed as their feelings of disappointment filled me, compounded by my own guilt. I understood all the suffering I had caused, and I felt it. I began to tremble. I saw how much grief my bad temper had caused, and I suffered this grief. I saw my selfishness, and my heart cried for relief. How had I been so uncaring?[1]

She also referred to the "ripple effect" of these actions:

> I saw how I had often wronged people and how they had turned to others and committed a similar wrong. The chain continued from victim to victim, like a circle of dominoes, until it came back to the start—to me, the offender . . . I had offended far more people than I knew, and my pain multiplied and became unbearable.[2]

At her time of greatest remorse, Eadie received comfort:

> Then I felt the love of the [spirit world] council come over me. They watched my life with understanding and mercy. Everything about me was taken into consideration, how I was raised, the things I had been taught, the pain given to me by others, the opportunities I had received or not received.[3]

Stated Robert Hugh Benson:

> So many in the spirit world are surprised when they discover that some small service that they have done—and immediately afterwards forgotten—has helped them in their spiritual progression to an extent that they could scarcely have thought possible.[4]

C. S. Lewis expressed eloquently the eternal significance of our relationship with others:

> It's a serious thing to live in a society of possible gods and goddesses, to remember that the dullest and most uninteresting person you talk to may one day be a creature which, if you saw it now, you would be strongly tempted to worship, or else a horror and a corruption such as you now meet, if at all, only in a nightmare. All day long we are, in some degree, helping each other to one or another of these destinations.[5]

President James E. Faust taught concerning our wrongs to others, "I believe the kind and merciful God, whose children we are, will judge us as lightly as He can for the wrongs we have done and give us the maximum blessings for the good we do."[6]

Concerning our potential for greater joy and happiness in the next life than can be attained on earth, Elder Orson Pratt, an early Apostle of the Church, taught:

> [There are those who] have never desired to injure any of the children of men, male or female. What do these reflections produce? They produce joy, satisfaction, peace, consolation, and this joy is a hundred-fold more intense than what the spirit is capable of perceiving or enjoying in this life . . . *Our spirits then will be happy, far*

more happy than what we are capable even of conceiving or having the least idea of in this world.[7] (italics added)

"The Preacher" said it well, "Cast thy bread upon the waters: for thou shalt find it after many days" (*Ecclesiastes 11:1*).

Spirit World Occupations

Benson taught, "This is no land of 'eternal rest.' There is rest in abundance for those who need it. But when the rest has restored them to full vigor and health, the urge to perform some sensible, useful task rises up within them, and opportunities abound."[8]

There is no occupation that requires what we call "toil."[9] And one can choose to change occupations as frequently as one cares to.[10] When a spirit is qualified to ascend to a higher realm, he or she is certain to find increased opportunities and responsibilities commensurate with his or her increased capacity.

Benson provides an example of transitioning from the various earthly occupations to spirit world professions:

> It might be said that most of us on the earth-plane have had a two-fold existence—our home life and the life connected with our business or occupation.
>
> In the latter, we associate, perhaps, with an entirely different group of people. It is therefore in the natural order of things, here in the spirit, that much the same state of things should also exist. The scientist, for example, will meet, first of all, his own family connections. When the question of work is broached, he will find himself among his old colleagues who have passed into the spirit world before him, and he will again feel more at home. And he will be more than overjoyed at the prospect of the scientific research that stretches before him.[11]

We have previously made reference to some of the occupations available in the spirit world (Benson states that there are thousands)[12], but we have yet to mention one of the primary ones—the sheer magnitude of ongoing spirit-world construction.

Necessitated by a constant influx of transitioning souls, there is a subsequent constant need of more housing, parks, gardens, and libraries. It appears that even in times of pestilence and war on earth, the prescience of the spirits in the upper realms begins construction before the pending disaster, precluding shortages.

Benson's example of a construction projects there provides a glimpse of the attitude of friendly cooperation present in all spirit world professions:

> [The architects] work for the sheer joy it brings them in the creation of some grand edifice to be used in the service of their fellows. These good men collaborate in a way that would be almost impossible in upon the earth-plane. Here they are not circumscribed by professional etiquette, or limited by the narrowness of petty jealousies. Each is more than happy and proud to serve with the other, and never is there discord or disagreement through endeavoring to introduce, or force, the individual ideas of the one at the expense of another's.... Whatever gifts we may possess in spirit, it is part of the essence of this realm that we have no inflated ideas of the power or excellence of those gifts. We acknowledge them in humility alone. . . .

He also explained the uniqueness of their building process:

> The masons, and one other, are the only people concerned in the actual construction, since spirit buildings do not require much that has to be included within the disposition of earthly buildings. Such, for example, as the necessary provision for lighting by artificial means, and for heating . . . light comes from the great central source of all light, and the warmth is one of the spiritual features of the realm . . . [The masons] had all the appearance of being extremely happy and jovial, and many were the jokes that circulated round this cheerful band.
>
> It must be remembered that the act of building in the spirit world is essentially an operation of thought. It will not be surprising, therefore, when I tell you that nowhere were there to be seen the usual materials and

paraphernalia associated with earthly builders, the scaffolding and bricks and cement, and the various other familiar objects. We were to witness, in fact, an act of creation—of creation by thought—and as such no "physical" equipment is necessary.

Spirit World Animals

Animals play a big part in most people's lives. Do these creatures go on to live in the spirit world? In D&C 77, the Prophet Joseph Smith explained portions of the Revelation of St. John. He said that in paradise, "[exists] the spirit of the beast and every other creature which God has created" (*vs. 3*).

Young Colton Burpo noted seeing "animals of every kind."[13] Later in the same book (*Heaven Is For Real*), he was more specific, mentioning . . . "horse[s] . . . dogs . . . birds, even a lion—and the lion was friendly, not fierce."[14] Additionally, Benson remarked that the seas are full of the signs of life.[15]

Birds

My wife loves birds. She spots birds I would never see, and she recognizes the species by their call. She loved our years in the tropics. So I dare not exclude a few notes about birds from this study.

Benson, Ruth, and Roger encountered beautiful birds while visiting an island together:

> But the great feature [was] the most wonderful birds, whose plumage presented a riot of color. Some of the birds were flying about, others—the larger variety—were walking majestically along the ground. But all of them were unafraid of us. They walked with us as we strolled along, and when we held up our hands, some small bird would perch upon our fingers. They seemed to know us, to know that any harm coming to them was an utter impossibility. They did not require to make a con-

stant search for food nor exercise a perpetual vigilance against what on earth would be their natural enemies.

They were, like ourselves, part of the eternal world of spirit, enjoying in their way, as we do in ours, their eternal life. Their very existence there was just another of those thousands of things that are given us for our delight.

The birds which had the most gorgeous plumage were evidently of the kind that live in the tropical parts of the earth-plane, and which are never seen by the eye of man until he comes to the spirit world. By the perfect adjustment of temperature, they are able to live in comfort with those of less-spectacular appearance. And all the time they were singing and twittering in a symphony of sound. It was never wearying, in spite of the quantity of sound that was going on, because in some extraordinary fashion the musical sounds blended with each other. Neither were they piercing in quality despite the fact that many of the small birds' songs were themselves high-pitched.[16]

Many NDEers speak of traveling through a tunnel in passage to the spirit world. Betty Eadie said of her experience in the tunnel, "I became aware of other people as well as animals traveling with me."[17]

Summarizing several NDEs, Brent Top stated, "Cattle, horses, sheep, and lions are mentioned."[18]

Sarah LaNell Menet noted the lack of insects in the realm she visited: "I did not see any insects in the spirit world. It was my understanding that when they cross over, they go to an entirely different place prepared just for them—a lower world, sort of a spirit world for insects."[19]

Sounds good to me!

Husbands and Wives

What about spouses—the ultimate and most intimate of associates? I found several accounts of greeting one's deceased spouse during the NDE. Benson taught, "There are many couples to be found living here; for example, a husband and wife who were happily married upon the earth, admirably suited to each other, and with a real bond of affection between them."[20]

What if two who were spouses in mortality qualify for different spirit-world realms? Benson provided a case in point:

> The wife passes into the spirit world and attains to a certain sphere. Later on, the husband in turn passes into spirit life, but goes to occupy a realm lower than that of his wife. But the mutual affection still exists, and so the wife takes up her life in the lower sphere in order to be with her husband and help him in his progression.[21]

In the NDE Rebecca Ruter Springer experienced shortly after the American Civil War, someone she supposed was the Savior reasoned with her concerning eternal marriage. Missing her "dear husband," she wrote:

> Suddenly a soft touch rested upon my bowed head, and a voice I had learned to recognize and love beyond all things in earth or heaven said: 'Have I not said truly, though he were dead, yet shall he live again?' (*John 11:25–26.*) 'What are now the years of separations, since the meeting again is at hand? Come, and let us reason a little together' the Master said, smiling down into my uplifted face. He took my extended hand into his own and sitting down beside me continued: 'Let us consider what these years have done for you. Do you not feel that you are infinitely better prepared to confer happiness than when you parted from him you love?'
> I nodded in glad affirmation. 'Do you not realize that you stand upon a higher plane, with more exalted ideas of life and its duties; and that, in the strength of the Father, you two hence forward will walk upward together?'
> Again, I gladly acquiesced. 'Is the life here less attractive than it was in the earth life?'
> 'No, no! A thousand times no,' I cried.
> 'Then there is nothing but joy in the reunion at hand?'

'Nothing but joy,' I echoed.

Then the Savior led me on to talk of the one so soon to come, and I opened my glad heart to him and told him of the noble life, the unselfish toil, the high aspirations, the unfaltering trust of him I loved. I spoke of his fortitude in misfortune, his courage in the face of sore trial and disappointment, his forgiveness of even malicious injury; and concluded by saying, 'He lived the Christianity many others professed. He always distanced me in that.'

The face of the Master glowed in sympathy as I talked, and when I had ceased, he said, 'I perceive that you have discovered the secret which makes marriage as eternal as the years of heaven.'

'Oh,' I said, 'to me, marriage must be eternal! How could it be otherwise when two grow together and become as one? Death cannot separate them without destroying; they are no longer two perfect beings, but one in soul and spirit forever.'

'Aye,' he answered, 'but having the marriage rite pronounced does not produce the change. It is the divinity of soul wedded to soul alone that can do that.'

So, he led me on until my soul flew upward as a lark in the early morning. He unfolded to me of the soul life that filled my heart with rapture, but which I may not here reveal.[22]

Although Benson mentioned but little about eternal family relationships, he said that "upon earth the number of generations of a family is fairly limited, but in the spirit world all previous generations of a family are co-existing."[23]

He also noted that when he passed through the veil, "there were . . . numbers of friends who were waiting to meet me again after our long separation."[24]

Families Are Forever

Eternal sociality with our loved ones is one of the primary aspects of the plan of salvation. In the Book of Mormon, Lehi teaches us that "men are that they might have joy" (*2 Nephi 2:25*). Man can experience full joy only when in the presence of those dearest to him.

When the resurrected Savior visited the land Bountiful in the Western Hemisphere, He blessed the people, brought the children close around Him, prayed to His Father, and "so great was the joy of the multitude that they were overcome" (*3 Nephi 17:18*). It was then that He expressed, "my joy is full" (*vs. 20*).

Lehi exemplified this in a dream recorded at the beginning of the Book of Mormon. Speaking of the tree of life, he said, "And it came to pass that I did go forth and partake of the fruit thereof; and I beheld that it was the most sweet, above all that I had ever before tasted. Yea, and I beheld that the fruit thereof was white, to exceed all the whiteness that I had ever seen" (*1 Nephi 8:11*). Then comes the most telling portion: "And as I partook of the fruit thereof it filled my soul with exceedingly great joy; wherefore, I began to be desirous that my family should partake of it also" (*vs. 12*).

Elder Jeffrey R. Holland recently expressed that an eternal mansion "could be no more to me than a decaying shack if my beloved Pat and our children were not with me to share that inheritance."[25] Joy comes only when shared with those we love. This extends beyond family to many others who are dear to us.

Some years ago, in association with a stake conference, Elder Holland was to have lunch with us in our home. We were delighted, but at the same time apprehensive. At that time, our mentally handicapped daughter Debbie was struggling with frequent severe seizures that would throw her into a rage, and she would literally attack anyone within range. (Most of our other children's friends were afraid to come to our home.) What if Debbie attacked Elder Holland?

We relished his visit to our home, and Debbie did not have a seizure while he was here. However, just as he walked out the door, she complained, and we thought, *Uh-oh, here comes the violence.* Instead, she clarified, "Not him go."

When someone dear to us passes on, we say within ourselves "Not him (or her) go," but a loving Father, through His only Begotten Son, has prepared for us a glorious post-mortal reunion, wherein we might eventually experience a fulness of joy.

NOTES

1. Eadie, Betty J., *Embraced by the Light*, 112.
2. Ibid., 113.
3. Ibid.
4. Borgia, Anthony, *Here and Hereafter*, 18.
5. Lewis, C. S., *Weight of Glory*, 1.
6. Faust, James E., "Woman, Why Weepest Thou?" General Conference, October 1996.
7. *Journal of Discourses*, vol. 2, 239–40.
8. Borgia, *Life in the World Unseen*, 110.
9. Ibid., 115–19.
10. Ibid., 170–1.
11. Ibid., 168.
12. Ibid.
13. Burpo, Todd, *Heaven is for Real*, 69.
14. Ibid., 152.
15. Borgia, *Here and Hereafter*, 94.
16. Ibid.
17. Eadie, 38.
18. Top, Brent L. and Wendy C., *Glimpses Beyond Death's Door*, 122.
19. Menet, Sarah LaNell, *There Is No Death*, 107.
20. Borgia, *Here and Hereafter*, 89.
21. Ibid., 90.
22. Springer, Rebecca Ruter, *My Dream of Heaven*, 118–19.
23. Borgia, *Here and Hereafter*, 87.
24. Borgia, *Life in the World Unseen*, 18.
25. Holland, Jeffrey R., "A Perfect Brightness of Hope," General Conference, October 2020.

Chapter 17
Learning in the Spirit World

> "It seemed that all of a sudden, all knowledge—of all that had started from the very beginning, that would go on without end—that for a second, I knew all the secrets of all ages, all the meaning of the universe, the stars, the moon—of everything...."
> — *Dr. Raymond Moody*

As mentioned in Chapter 7 (Progress in the Spirit World), learning in the spirit world will be exponentially easier and faster—It's one of the things I'm looking forward to the most.

Whatever your physical brain has forgotten in this life lives on in the mind and is regained after mortality.[1]

Thirst for Knowledge

The desire to attain knowledge is apparently stronger post-mortally. This may be related to the desire to progress to a higher realm. Said Joseph Smith, "A man is saved no faster than he gains knowledge."[2]

One NDEer expressed it as "a burning thirst for knowledge."[3]

Robert Hugh Benson explained, "The pursuit of knowledge is far greater than upon the earth-plane, since the necessity of turning our minds to the pressing need and exigencies of incarnate life no longer exist [there]."[4]

Benson also instructed us that the realm assignment in the spirit world is not contingent alone upon the knowledge one acquires in mortality. To me this reflects the justice of a loving God.

Some have mental handicaps or learning disabilities. One of our daughters has a severe mental handicap that prevents her from comprehending above the three- or four-year-old level. Others lived, or now live, with little exposure to education, lacking even the opportunity to acquire basic literacy. Others' circumstances may have demanded, or even now demand, full-time attention to the essentials of existence. God's plan includes mercy and opportunity for all mankind.

All Knowledge

From his research, Dr. Raymond Moody reported that some NDEers experience a "vision of knowledge." Stated one whom he interviewed:

> It seemed that all of a sudden, all knowledge—of all that had started from the very beginning, that would go on without end—that for a second, I knew all the secrets of all ages, all the meaning of the universe, the stars, the moon—of everything ... It was in all forms of communication, sights, sounds, thoughts. It was any—and everything. It was as if there was nothing that wasn't known. All knowledge was there, not just one field, but everything.[5]

Betty J. Eadie believes that she had one-on-one "tutoring" by the Savior Himself. She wrote:

> His light now began to fill my mind, and my questions were answered even before I fully asked them. His light was knowledge ... The answers were absolute and complete ... Things were coming back to me from long before my life on earth ... I could understand volumes in an instant. It was as if I could look at a book and comprehend it at a glance—as though I could just sit back while the book revealed itself to me in every detail, forward

and backward, inside and out, every nuance and possible suggestion, all in an instant.

As I comprehended one thing, more questions and answers would come to me, all building on each other, and interacting as if all truth were intrinsically connected. The word "omniscient" had never been more meaningful to me.[6]

Of course, these two had only a glimpse of the environment where all knowledge exists. They did not receive and retain all knowledge; they were merely momentarily exposed to it. Were it not so, what a huge advantage they would possess when returning to mortality!

Assisted Learning

From her NDE, Dr. Mary C. Neal learned (just as Benson expressed) that gaining knowledge in the spirit world is facilitated because there is 'life," or "animation," in everything, and that life "shares" knowledge.[7]

Duane Crowther quoted one NDEer as saying, "We're able to absorb knowledge by holding or touching, seeing, [or] being close to something."[8]

Continued Learning

Let's not forget that most NDEers have visited only one realm. Benson purports to visiting several. Said he of knowledge and learning: "There are many, many things there that we do not understand—and it will take eons of time before we even have a faint gleam of understanding them."[9]

He also declared:

> While we are incarnate our vision is limited—very limited . . . In the next life we are upon rising ground where our vision is less restricted and our outlook is wider, more comprehensive, and where we can draw in full measure upon the many wise minds that dwell there.[10]

They literally see much of the "big picture" that is unavailable to mortals.

Students

When we hear the word "student" or "pupil," we tend to surmise it means young people. In the next life, the students are in, or evolving toward, the prime of life. They may have inhabited the spirit world for moments or millennia. Learning is co-eternal with life itself.

Benson, Ruth, and Edwin visited a spirit-world school. Explained Benson, "The joy of these students is great in their freedom from their earthly restrictions and bodily limitations. Here instruction is easy, and the acquisition and application of knowledge is simple for those who wish to learn."

Benson further observed that, for students in the next life:

> Gone are all the struggles of the student in surmounting of earthly difficulties both of the mind and of the hands, and progress towards proficiency is consequently smooth and rapid. The happiness of all the students we saw, itself spread happiness to all who beheld it, for there is no limit to their endeavors when that bugbear of earthly life—fleeting time—and all the petty vexations of the mundane existence have been abandoned forever . . . it was a school where souls, who had had the misfortune to miss the benefits of some earthly knowledge and learning, could help here equip themselves intellectually.[11]

What a wonderful delight awaits our mentally handicapped daughter, and all of God's children who have struggled through life with a serious malady.

Benson expounds:

> Knowledge and learning, education and erudition do not connote spiritual worth, and the inability to read and write do not imply the absence of it . . . We found in this school many souls busy with their studies, and thoroughly enjoying themselves. To acquire knowledge here is not

> tedious, because the memory works perfectly—that is, unfailingly—and the powers of mental perception are no longer hampered and confined by the human brain.
>
> Our facilities for understanding are sharpened, and intellectual expansion is sure and steady. The school was the home of realized ambitions to most of the students within it. I chatted with a number of them, and each told me that what he was studying now, he had longed to study on earth, but he had been denied the opportunity for reasons that are all too familiar. Some had found that commercial activities had left no time, or that the struggle for a living had absorbed all the means to do so.
>
> The school was very comfortably arranged; there was, of course, no hint of regimentation. Each student followed his own course of study independently of anyone else. He seated himself comfortably, or he went to the lovely gardens without. He began when he wanted, and he finished when he wanted, and the more he dipped into his studies the more interested and fascinated he became.[12]

Spirit world learning often includes a laboratory, not just a classroom. In these labs they practice, experiment, add proficiency, or even fail in some ventures.[13] (Unlike here on earth, there are no disastrous consequences to failure).

Teachers

There are superb teachers in the spirit world. Benson gives us details on their service. He wrote:

> Edwin [his guide] pointed out to us the dwelling places of many of the teachers in the various halls of learning, who preferred to live close to the seats of their work . . . Edwin said that we should always be welcome should we ever wish to call on any of the teachers. The exclusiveness which must necessarily surround such people when they are incarnate vanishes when they come into the spirit [world]. All values become drastically altered in such matters.

> The teachers themselves do not cease their own studies because they are teaching. They are ever investigating and learning and passing on to their pupils what they have thus gained.
>
> Some have progressed to a higher realm, but they still retain their interest in their former sphere, and continuously visit it—and their many friends—to pursue their teaching.[14]

Benson says teachers must be proficient in both the conceptual and the practical. There are needs or necessary skills in the spirit world that require both instruction and practice to become proficient.[15] Examples include traveling at high speed and to different times. These are beyond the scope of this study; we will learn soon enough, and until we make that transition, we have no need to know.

Libraries

Several NDEers mentioned the great libraries in the spirit world. In fact, there are entire cities dedicated to diverse learning centers. Benson calls them "temples" in which spirit people learn about innumerable subjects, yet each one of these people acknowledges "the eternal thanks that we owe to the Great Father."[16] Because the books have their own animation, they "respond" to the inquirer.

Dr. Moody, from his research, learned that in the spirit world should someone focus on any particular thing, knowledge would "flow" from that object to the inquirer.[17] A non-reader can apparently be "tutored" by the book itself, through his or her thoughts (perhaps similar to how the Holy Spirit communicates to mortals).

Benson mentioned the option of actually reading books, as opposed to receiving the knowledge in the other available ways. In the same vein, Crowther related an NDE that suggests that in the spirit world one often reads conventionally when doing so for pleasure.[18] Apparently, we will still be able to relax, snuggle up, and get lost in a good book.

Multimedia

NDEers reference many means of communication: speaking the many languages of the earth, mental telepathy (which sometimes includes understanding a person's intents and feelings), receiving knowledge merely from pondering an issue, totally comprehending an object just from touching it, seeing in vision what another person is describing (similar to Moroni's description of the Hill Cumorah appearing in Joseph Smith's mind, as recounted in the Joseph Smith History in the Pearl of Great Price), even speaking a pure language, in which a person can express perfectly his or her intent or message with no possibility for misunderstanding. Emanuel Swedenborg declared that this "pure" language (perhaps the Adamic language?) was spoken only in the highest realm.[19]

Some Final Points

Some NDEers have stated that light and knowledge are synonymous[20] and that knowledge plus experience equals intelligence.[21] This last observation reminds me of the Mark Twain axiom: "The most permanent lessons in [life] are those which come, not by booky teaching, but of experience. A man who carries a cat by the tail learns something he can learn in no other way."[22]

Rachel's Experience

> While visiting the spirit world, I had the ability to learn and communicate perfectly through the Holy Ghost. The clarity of knowledge was immense, the acquisition eternal. Though this explanation may sound quite overwhelming, it was truly the opposite. All information seemed simple and non-threatening to learn.

I experienced this sacred process of gaining and exchanging information with far more certainty than I had ever thought possible. Gram and I spoke nonverbally, yet our discussions were completely clear. The experience far exceeded mind-reading trickery, rather approached the understanding that comes with the testifying power of the Holy Ghost. My understanding of her was so utterly clear, so precise, that we quickly agreed on how to resolve my circumstances.

I had never before experienced the ease of understanding another with such exactness. I was not only vividly aware of her thoughts but also her views and opinions. Interestingly, it wasn't necessary for her to speak out loud, but I did need her consent to discover what she wished to share.

NOTES

1. Crowther, Duane S., *Life Everlasting: A Definitive Study of Life After Death*, 215.
2. Smith, Joseph Fielding (compiler), *Teachings of the Prophet Joseph Smith*, 217.
3. Crowther, 213.
4. Borgia, Anthony, *Life in the World Unseen*, (dictated by Robert Hugh Benson), 48.
5. Moody, Raymond, 148-149.
6. Eadie, Betty J., *Embraced by the Light*, 44-45.
7. Neal, Mary C., *To Heaven and Back*, 102.
8. Crowther, 216.
9. Borgia, 33.
10. Ibid., 124.
11. Ibid.
12. Ibid., 46.
13. Ibid., 47.
14. Ibid., 48.
15. Ibid., 51.
16. Ibid.
17. Moody, 151.

18. Crowther, 221.
19. Quoted in Top, Brent L. and Wendy C., *Glimpses Beyond Death's Door*, 64.
20. Crowther, 217.
21. Ibid, 213.
22. Harnsberger, Caroline Thomas (compiler), *Mark Twain at Your Fingertips: A Book of Quotations*, p. 110.

Wesley M. White

Chapter 18
The Spirits of Children

> "A child who has passed on to the next life is comforted and loved and in no way suffers but will experience an increased joy and happiness, beyond description, when reunited with his or her own mother."
>
> — *Rachel Andersen*

There is evidence that children, at least for a time, maintain their child stature in the spirit world. The Church's October 1929 issue of the magazine, *The Improvement Era*, included a near-death experience by Sister Ellen Jensen. While on the other side, she witnessed a group of "hundreds of children" singing under the direction of Eliza R. Snow.

A few days before Emma Hale Smith's death (nearly thirty-five years after her husband Joseph Smith's martyrdom), she told her nurse, Elizabeth Revel, that Joseph had come to her in a vision. Emma reported that he said to her:

> 'Come with me, it is time for you to come with me.' I put on my bonnet and my shawl and went with him. I did not think that it was anything unusual. I went with him into a mansion, and he showed me through the different departments of that beautiful mansion.

Elizabeth Revel then narrated:

> And one room was a nursery. In that nursery was a babe in the cradle. [Emma] said, 'I know my babe, my

Don Carlos that was taken from me.' She sprang forward, caught the child up in her arms, and wept with joy over the child. When Emma recovered herself sufficiently, she turned to Joseph and said, 'Joseph, where are the rest of my children?' He said to her, 'Emma, be patient and you shall have all of your children.' Then she saw standing by his side a personage of light, even the Lord Jesus Christ.[1]

One NDEer, when describing spirit world libraries, mentioned "groups of children [who] came running across the lawn with their teacher."[2]

Dr. Eban Alexander observed "children . . . laughing and playing."[3]

Emanuel Swedenborg proclaimed that children:

> . . . are borne into heaven and entrusted to angels of the feminine gender who during their physical life had loved children tenderly and also loved God. Because they had in the world loved all children with a virtually maternal tenderness, they accept these as their own. And the children, from their inborn nature, love them as though they were their own mother. Each woman has as many children as she wants from her spiritual parental affection . . . Once this stage is completed, they are transferred to another.[4]

Swedenborg also described how these spirit children eventually become adults:

> Understanding and wisdom constitute an angel. Just as long as these children do not possess these attributes, they are with angels but are not themselves angels. But once they become understanding and wise, they become angels. Further—which surprised me—they do not look like children, but like adults. For at that point, they are no longer of a childlike nature, but of a more mature, angelic nature . . . The reason that children look more mature as they become more perfect in understanding and wisdom is that understanding and wisdom are spiritual nourishment itself . . . Children in heaven do not

The Spirits of Children

mature beyond the beginning of young adulthood and remain at that point to eternity.[5]

The dream that President Joseph F. Smith had while a teenage missionary serving in Hawaii is well known to members of the Church. He dreamt that he visited the spirit world. There, the Prophet Joseph Smith told him he was late, and young Joseph replied, "Yes, but I am clean." In that same vision, Joseph F. Smith reported that he saw his mother, Mary Fielding Smith, and that "she sat with a child in her lap."[6]

Robert Hugh Benson provides more detail of children who have passed on:

> What of the souls that pass over as children; indeed, what of those, even, who pass into the spirit world at birth? The answer is that they grow as they would have grown upon the earth-plane. But the children here—of all ages—are given such treatment and care as would never be possible in the earth world. The young child, whose mind is not yet fully formed, is uncontaminated by earthly contacts, and on passing into the spirit world it finds itself in a realm of great beauty, presided over by souls of equal beauty. The children's realm has been called the 'nursery of heaven.'[7]

Benson explains:

> The children's realm is a township in itself, containing everything that great minds, inspired by the greatest Mind, could possibly provide for the welfare, comfort and education, and the pleasure and happiness of its youthful inhabitants.[8]

They abide in:

> ... the quaintest little cottages such as one was always inclined to believe only belonged to the pages of children's story books.... Great numbers of children live in these tiny dwellings, each being presided over by an older child, who is perfectly capable of attending to any situation that might arise.[9]

He said that those selected to teach these children "all undergo an extensive training course before they are judged fit to fill the post of teacher to the children, and to conform with, and uphold, the rigidly high standards of the work."[10]

He described the children as all ages, from "those who had been born dead, to the youth of sixteen or seventeen years of earth time."[11]

Benson also explained that "the mental and physical growth of the child in the spirit world is much more rapid than in the earth world."[12]

The "ruler" of the realm acts, in a general sense, as if he were their parent, and the children look up to him as a father. They are taught primarily spiritual things, and some parts of earthly curriculum, with many parts of the latter omitted as superfluous.[13]

A close friend often says that his assignment of choice after this life would be to work with little children who had been abused in mortality, giving them all the love and attention possible to accelerate their healing. Perhaps he may get his wish.

A Mother's Sacrifice

A rather unusual NDE may be of some comfort to those who have lost a child. Shortly after the delivery of her daughter, a new mother who had "died" was visited by a spirit who took her by her right hand:

> When he took hold of my hand, I immediately knew him to be the greatest friend I had. I also knew that I was a very special person to him. The thrill of this touch of hands exceeds anything I have experienced on earth, in life as we know it. Our meeting was 'understood'—sensed—not visual. He told me he had 'come for my child.' 'My child?' I asked, scarcely able to contain my joy and happiness over the news that one of my own children would be going back with him! It was, I 'knew' a very high honor to be selected for this. I had the honor of

being the mother of a very extra-special child, and I was so proud that he had picked my child.[14]

The being told her:

'I will return for your child in four days.' Four days later, when she was signing her discharge papers it was apparent that something very consequential had occurred: 'The nurse was devastated. She knew Tari was dead and I didn't. 'Oh, God,' she wailed, 'your doctor should have been here by now! I'm not supposed to tell you, but I can't let you go on believing that Tari is alive. She died early this morning.'[15]

The mother continued:

In the weeks following, I felt no grief for my own loss, but I felt sorry for my friends and relatives who didn't know where Tari was, and couldn't believe—really believe—that my 'experience' was anything more than a vivid dream . . . Well, I soon realized that my acceptance back into this world depended upon 'pretending' to forget, and 'pretending' to grieve the loss of my baby. So, I did this for everybody else's sake—except my husband, who believed me, and gained some comfort from it, second-hand.[16]

A Child's NDE

Now let us look at an NDE from the innocent view of a child. You may wish to refer to the book *Heaven Is for Real* (or perhaps you have seen the movie). The four-year-old son of the author, a pastor named Todd Burpo, experiences an NDE and comes back with information contrary to much of his father's ecclesiastical training, but largely in harmony with the restored gospel.

Young Colton Burpo said that "there were many, many children in heaven."[18] One day out of the blue he said to his mother, Sonja, "Mommy, I have two sisters."[19] His mother explained that he had but one sister, Cassie, and that perhaps he was including his cousin. Colton replied, "I have two sisters. You had a baby die in your tummy." When Sonja asked who told him that, he replied, "She did, Mommy. She said she died in your tummy."

Todd, Colton's father, explained that losing that baby was the most painful event of Sonja's life. Although they had told Cassie, they felt Colton was too young. As Colton saw the tears in his mother's eyes, he said, "She's okay, God adopted her." In conformity with her religious training, Sonja asked Colton, "Don't you mean Jesus adopted her?" Colton replied, "No, Mommy. His Dad did."[17]

Colton's childlike explanation harmonizes well with what my wife Kay felt when we lost a son in her second trimester. She feels that the fetus had a spirit, that the time of pregnancy was his mortality, and that if we are faithful, we shall have both him and his deceased brother, Russell, in our eternal family.

I have pondered extensively Emanual Swedenborg's and Benson's explanations of childcare being provided by loving spirits, but with little mention of family. Could this be because their experiences took place in a middle realm? I suppose that in paradise the care of infants is gladly conducted by deceased family members, many of whom have covenant ties to these children. Another possibility is that the township spoken of by Benson was not their home or permanent dwelling any more than a school is the permanent home of the attendees. I also suppose that the "hundreds of children" being taught music by Eliza R. Snow were attending a music class taught by her and that most were not under her permanent care.

Further, Swedenborg and Benson are both male bachelors, without the sacred and intimate sentiments of womanhood and motherhood. If a woman were to give a description of a child's spirit world circumstance, I believe we would see a more tender, sensitive, and detailed perspective.

The Spirits of Children

If this chapter had to be reduced to one sentence, it might be: God and the Savior—and multitudes of special women—love and care for little children on both sides of the veil.

Rachel's Experience

As nothing compares to the revered love between a mother and her child, this relationship is also preserved beyond comparison in the spirit world. This bond is irreplaceable. A child who has passed on to the next life is comforted and loved and in no way suffers but will experience an increased joy and happiness, beyond description, when reunited with his or her own mother.

NOTES

1. Smith, Lucy Mack, *The Revised and Enhanced History of Joseph Smith by His Mother*, 451–52.
2. Crowther, Duane S., *Life Everlasting: A Definitive Study of Life After Death*, 219.
3. Alexander, Eben, *Proof of Heaven*, 65–6.
4. Top, Brent L. and Wendy C., *Glimpses Beyond Death's Door*, 214.
5. Ibid., 215.
6. Crowther, 183.
7. Borgia, Anthony, *Life in the World Unseen*, 155–56.
8. Ibid., 161.
9. Ibid., 157–58.
10. Ibid., 159.
11. Ibid.
12. Ibid., 160.
13. Ibid.
14. Ring, Kenneth, *Heading Toward Omega*, 77–8.
15. Ibid.
16. Ibid., 80–81.
17. Burpo, Todd, *Heaven is for Real*, 146.

Chapter 19
How the Spirit Differs From the Body

> "I thirst no more, I want to sleep no more, I hunger no more, I tire no more, I run, I walk, I labor ... nothing like pain or weariness. I am full of life, full of vigor."
> — *President John Taylor*

In Chapter 9, we talked of the higher realms of the spirit world, and I quoted President Brigham Young's vision or NDE. As an introduction to this chapter, I include a portion of that previous quote:

> I have had to exercise a great deal more faith to desire to live than I ever experienced in my whole life to live. The brightness and glory of the next apartment is inexpressible ... [In mortality] when we advance in years we have to be stubbing along and be careful lest we fall.
>
> But yonder how different! They move with ease and like lightning ... If we want to behold Jerusalem as it was in the days of the Savior; or if we want to see the Garden of Eden as it was when created, there we are, and we see it as it existed spiritually, for it was created first spiritually and then temporally, and spiritually it still remains. And when there we may visit any city we please that exists upon its surface.
>
> If we wish to understand how they are living here on these western islands, or in China, we are there; in fact, we are like the light of the morning ... We have the Father to speak to us, Jesus to speak to us, and angels to speak to

us and we shall enjoy the society of the just and the pure who are in the spirit world until the resurrection.[1]

President John Taylor echoed:

> [Death,] this dark shadow and valley so trifling; [one is] passed from a state of sorrow [and] grief . . . into a state of existence where I can enjoy life to the fullest extent as far as can be done without a body. . . I thirst no more, I want to sleep no more, I hunger no more, I tire no more, I run, I walk, I labor . . . nothing like pain or weariness. I am full of life, full of vigor.[2]

Young Colton Burpo declared that he had an encounter with "Pop" (his paternal grandfather) in the spirit world. Colton's father then brought out a photo of his father and showed it to Colton. Colton's dad expected him to light up in recognition. Instead, he frowned and shook his head, declaring, "Dad, nobody's old in heaven, and nobody wears glasses."[3]

Later, Colton's father located a photo of Pops when he was twenty-nine years old. When he showed it to Colton, Colton said happily, "How did you get a picture of Pops?"[4]

The "curse" of "eating [our] bread by the sweat of [our] brow," as well as the other arduous things President Taylor mentioned, will be forever gone, allowing us to give much more attention to the things of the kingdom. Our health will be perfect. We will evolve to our physical prime, with no blemishes.[5]

According to Moody's research, the human spirit has density but not "earthly density."[6] We will have the capacity to pass through earthly obstacles.[7]

Furthermore, gravity will not be a detriment to spirits. It will still be a necessary force for much of the environment, such as rivers and streams, yet traveling by foot you may still walk your (spirit) dog with no stress or body weight.[8]

In many realms, our clothing will be partially composed of light (and therefore, of truth).[9]

In at least the higher realms, travel, which requires so much time and effort on earth, can be instantaneous or slow, as we choose,[10] making the vastness of each spirit realm easily manageable.

The Immortal Mind

Let's turn our attention to the mind, freed from the constraints of the mortal brain.

Dr. Eben Alexander is a highly experienced neurosurgeon. His academic preparation encompassed forty years. Although he had attended church as a youth, he completely bought into academia, depending exclusively on physical evidence for knowledge. When his dying patients envisioned seeing a deceased loved one who invited the patient to pass on, or perhaps expressed a spiritual reassurance of a life beyond, Dr. Alexander was glad for the comfort provided to the patient but gave no credence to these experiences because of the lack of physical evidence. He explained that "modern neuroscience dictates that the brain gives rise to consciousness— to the mind, to the soul, to the spirit, to whatever you choose to call that invisible, intangible part of us that truly makes us who we are—and I had little doubt that it was correct."[11]

His life was devoid of anything spiritual; that is, until he "died."

His attending physicians, who included dear friends, were baffled by the disease that put Dr. Alexander into a coma, but they were no more confounded than he, who was experiencing an NDE. After his physical recovery, Alexander declared, "Everything I had learned in four decades of study and work about the human brain, about the universe, and about what constitutes reality conflicted with what I'd experienced during those seven days in a coma."[12]

He was particularly amazed by how much the marvelous human brain actually bridled the human mind. Our physical eyes, in conjunction with our brain, provide the miracle of vision. However, the mind, when unencumbered by the eyes and brain, can "see" in every direction, all the time. As marvelous as it is that our ears and brain cooperate to provide hearing, for the unrestricted mind, sound and sight are actually one in the same, in perfect harmony with all of our senses. Dr. Alexander realized that the brain is "a kind of reducing valve or filter, shifting the larger, nonphysical consciousness that we possess in the nonphysical worlds down into a more limited capacity for the duration of our mortal lives."[13]

For Dr. Alexander's unfettered mind, knowledge was omnipresent:

> Each time I silently posed [a question], the answer came instantly in an explosion of light, color, love and beauty that blew through me like a crashing wave.
> What was important about these bursts was that they didn't simply silence my questions by overwhelming them. They answered them, but in a way that bypassed language. Thoughts entered me directly. But it wasn't thought like we experience on earth. It wasn't vague, immaterial, or abstract. These thoughts were solid and immediate—hotter than fire and wetter than water—and as I received them, I was able to instantly and effortlessly understand concepts that would have taken me years to fully grasp in my earthly life.[14]

Robert Hugh Benson said, "In the spirit world we have no physical brain to hamper us, and our minds are fully and completely retentive of all knowledge that comes to us."[15] Benson additionally noted:

> I discovered that my mind was a veritable storehouse of facts concerning my earthly life. Every act I had performed, and every word that I had uttered, every impression I had reached; every fact that I had read about, and every incident I had witnessed, all these, I found, were indelibly registered in my subconscious mind.[16]

You will have all the knowledge you attained in mortality that "escaped" your mortal brain.

You will not only recollect every event, but you will also remember the associated emotions and feelings of those events. And you will be aware of how your words and deeds affected others.

As mentioned in Chapter 6, Dr. Mary C. Neal said of her life review:

> I was shown events in my life, not in isolation, but in the context of their unseen ripple effects . . . to see the impact of events or words dozens of times removed was profoundly powerful . . . I was able to clearly see that every action, every decision, and every human interaction impacts the bigger world in far more significant ways than we could ever be capable of appreciating.[17]

As included in Chapter 17, under "Continued Learning," Benson reported:

> While we are incarnate our vision is limited—very limited. . . [those in the next life] have advanced a little further along the road than have you, and . . . are upon rising ground where [their] vision is less restricted and [their] outlook is wider, more comprehensive, and where [they] can draw in full measure upon the many wise minds who dwell here.[18]

They literally see much of the "big picture" that is unavailable to mortals.

Elder Orson Pratt taught:

> Every act of our lives will be fresh upon the memory . . . It is not the want of capacity in the spirit of man that causes him to forget the knowledge he may have learned yesterday; but it is because of the imperfection of the tabernacle in which the spirit dwells . . . It is, then, this memory that will produce the suffering and the pains upon that class of spirits whose works have been wicked and abominable in the sight of God.[19]

The immortal mind can comprehend volumes of information in an instant.[20] Many NDEers have reported this ability to think more lucidly and rapidly.[21] They also report that it is as if they have additional senses. One Church-member NDEer stated, "[They] are able to absorb knowledge by holding or simply touching, seeing, being close to something . . . [They] in essence absorb knowledge through every part of [their] bodies."[22]

Reported another NDEer:

> All you would have to do is show me [a] tape recorder and I would be able to comprehend everything about it, instantly, even if I had never seen one before. My ability to comprehend and learn had been multiplied a thousand times or more. The slow, clunky manner in which I learned on earth had evaporated. I could absorb and comprehend things I had never thought possible. [23]

In this life, we miscommunicate frequently, causing misunderstanding and even bad feelings. In the spirit world, some sort of telepathy makes misunderstanding impossible. In Raymond Moody's *The Light Beyond*, a spirit-world guide explained this difference to a man experiencing an NDE:

> For instance, if I told you that I wanted to meet you in the park, you'd want to know what park, where in the park, an exact location. I would use words to describe everything the way I understood them. You might not have the same definition for the words I chose. Therefore, a misunderstanding (sic). But, if I sent a message telepathically to you of the same park, you'd see the exact spot of the park I had chosen.[24]

Benson and others have said that when spirits communicate mind to mind, even the associated emotions are shared perfectly. He calls these "thought links."[25]

Emanuel Swedenborg professed that in the highest realm, the inhabitants speak in a purer and more beautiful language and that "angels can know a person's whole life from the tone, from a few spoken words."[26] Perhaps this is the Adamic language (see *Moses 6:5–6*).

Some may feel uncomfortable with the idea of "broadcasting" our thoughts. Swedenborg explained:

> Your thoughts are private. If you need to communicate with someone, then you project out to someone, or to a group, or to everyone here. When you are only thinking to yourself, your mind has a way of shutting out or shielding itself from thought leakage.[27]

Anatomy and Physiology of Our Spirits

Benson teaches us some spirit world anatomy and physiology in his book, *Here and Hereafter* (dictated to Anthony Borgia). He reiterates the relationship of the mind to the mortal brain: "There are many things that we have to unlearn and re-learn when we first come to dwell in the spirit lands, but our minds, being then free of a heavy physical brain, are at liberty to exercise their powers to the full."[28]

The mind can quickly learn, living in these very different conditions of existence, how to enhance one's capacities by abiding by spiritual laws. For example, for a spirit, mere thoughts are a powerful mode to accomplish something. After sufficient study and practice, a spirit can travel immense distances quickly and accurately. No spirit is ever "lost in the woods." A spirit can create ("organize from matter unorganized" may be a better expression) a building, a city, a research facility, a garden, a library, a temple, or much more just by applying the powerful thought processes that he has studied, practiced, and learned. This process seems to align well with the scriptural accounts of the Creation.

With this great power of thought, we might suppose that our hands would then be useless. Benson explains why this isn't true:

> Because we can create so much with our minds, because we can fabricate things by the close application

> of thought, then, it might be imagined that there is precious little left for our hands to do ... The truth is that we use our hands in a thousand different actions during what you would call the day's work ... For example, in our spirit homes we pick up a book; we open or close a door; we shake hands with some friend who calls; we arrange some flowers upon the table; we paint a picture or play upon a musical instrument, or we may operate a scientific apparatus of some sort ... We like to employ our hands in conjunction with our minds ... There are plenty of things that could be created in these realms purely by thought and without the least interposition of hands, but we like to go the long way round sometimes and find some employment for our hands .... [29]

He said that it is much the same with our feet: "We like to walk just as we used to upon earth."[30] Spirit beings are capable of walking hundreds of miles with no fatigue, but for greater distances, they generally "think" themselves there, as previously discussed.

Monsignor Benson taught that spirits "breathe ... The spirit world has air just as you have on earth, and we have lungs in our bodies with which to breathe it. And it does 'reinvigorate' the blood [or the fluid in our veins] in what would be the spirit world equivalent of that process ... Our blood [or the substance that replaces it] is reinvigorated by the spiritual force and energy that is one of the principal constituents of the air we breathe here."[31]

Unlike mortals, spirits have no requirement for food or drink:

> We derive another part of our sustenance from the light of these realms, from the abundance of color, from the water, from the fruit when we wish to eat of it, from the flowers, and from all that is beautiful itself, ... but we also take strength from the great spiritual force that is being constantly poured down upon us from the Father of Heaven Himself.[32]

Personally, I suspect that this force is at least part of what the scriptures call the "Light of Christ."

NOTES

1. BYU Press, *Teachings of Presidents of the Church: Brigham Young*, Priesthood/Relief Society manual, 282–283.
2. Quoted in Maxwell, *The Promise of Discipleship*, 106.
3. Burpo, Todd, *Heaven Is for Real*, 21.
4. Ibid., 22.
5. Borgia, Anthony, *Life in the World Unseen*, 152.
6. Moody, Raymond, *Life after Life*, 48.
7. Ibid., 34; and also in Top, *Glimpses Beyond Death's Door*, 41.
8. Crowther, Duane S., *Life Everlasting: A Definitive Study of Life After Death*, 200.
9. Top, Brent L. and Wendy C., *Glimpses Beyond Death's Door*, 48.
10. Moody, 38.
11. Alexander, Eben, *Proof of Heaven*, 59.
12. Ibid., 218.
13. Ibid., 125.
14. Alexander, 76.
15. Borgia, *Life in the World Unseen*, 130.
16. Borgia, *Life in the World Unseen*, 150.
17. Neal, Mary C., *To Heaven and Back*, 57.
18. Borgia, *Life in the World Unseen*, 150.
19. *Journal of Discourses*, vol. 2, 239–40.
20. Crowther, 44.
21. Moody, 37.
22. Crowther, 216.
23. Crowther, 214.
24. Moody, *The Light Beyond*, 45.
25. Borgia, 180.
26. Quoted in Top, 67.
27. Ibid.
28. Borgia, *Here and Hereafter*, 105.
29. Ibid., 106.
30. Ibid.
31. Ibid., 109.
32. Ibid., 111.

Wesley M. White

Chapter 20
Freedom From Frustration

> "And I soon go to the place of my rest, which is with my Redeemer; for I know that in him I shall rest. And I rejoice in the day when my mortal shall put on immortality, and shall stand before him; then shall I see his face with pleasure, and he will say unto me: Come unto me, ye blessed, there is a place prepared for you in the mansions of my Father. Amen."
> — *Enos 1:27*

We have already discussed many earthly challenges that do not exist in the spirit world, such as illness and tribulation. This chapter enumerates a few of the earthly frustrations that do not exist in at least the middle and higher realms of the spirit world.

Robert Hugh Benson stated that there is no hustle, bustle, or hurrying. Time is measured differently, and one has much more control over it. Transportation, after proper study and practice, can be instantaneous.[1] It is impossible to "waste time." "Nobody ever wasted time here, because there is no time to waste."[2] Benson also taught the following:

- There are no recurring seasons.[3]
- There is no boredom, loneliness, depression, anxiety, pain, suffering, calamities, accidents, discomfort, illness (mental, physical, nor emotional), fear, fatigue, confinement (except to one's spacious realm), self-consciousness,

unhappiness, unpleasantness, discord, discomfort, discontentment;[4] the list could go on and on.
- Many earthly occupations are not required: police officers, lawyers, medical personnel, firemen, psychologists, diplomats, and many others. In fact, my previous profession as a military pilot would fall into this category.
- There are no compass points (north, south, east, west). Destinations are seen in the mind prior to travel, and spirits have the inherent ability to arrive precisely there (after practice and training) without external references.[5]
- There are no national boundaries. One is free to travel anywhere within the spacious confines of one's realm.[6]
- There is no commerce: no bartering, buying, nor selling. However, there is "earning" and "ownership."[7]

Benson explains:

> There is ownership in the spirit world. Indeed, why should there not be? Ownership, however, is gained in a different way from that of the earth. There is only one right of ownership in the spirit world, and that is the spiritual right. None other will suffice; none other even exists. According to our spiritual right, gained by the kind of life we have lived upon earth, and afterwards according to our progression in the spirit world, so can we possess.[8]

He offered his home as an example:

> When the day shall dawn upon which [one's] spiritual progression will carry [him] onward, he shall leave his house. But it will rest entirely with [him] whether [he] leaves his old home as it stands for others to occupy and enjoy, or whether [he] demolishes it. It is customary, I am told, to make a gift of it to the ruler of the realm for his disposal to others at his discretion.[9]

Benson further explained:

> It's not by any means necessary for everyone who owns a house [there]. Some people don't want to be

bothered with one—though bothered is not the exact word to use, as no home, whether large or small, can possibly be a bother in any earthly sense.

But there are folk who don't feel the necessity for a house, and so they don't have one. Perfectly simple. To begin with, the sun is always shining in these and other regions, there's no unpleasant wind or cold.

It's always the same steady, unvarying genial warmth. . . . So there is nothing from which we need protection as on earth, in the way of the elements. As for privacy, well, there are myriads of spots . . . that will provide all the solitude you are likely to want.[10]

Clothes like the ones a spirit wore in mortality are available.[11] It makes sense that when a spirit is allowed to show him or herself to a mortal, they are dressed in clothes that the visitant recognizes; it could be considered an additional mode of identification. Benson explains that a spirit soon chooses to change to the comfortable, shimmering, animated robes of the spirit world.[12]

Speaking of other earthly possessions not required in the spirit world, Benson clarified:

Many people arrive here to find themselves richly and abundantly provided with spirit-world possessions that are far in excess of those which they owned upon the earth. And the contrary is often the case. Possessors of great earthly effects can find themselves spiritually poor when they come here. But they can gain the right to possess more, far more than they ever could own on earth, and of far greater value and beauty.[13]

He added, "In an idle moment you could compile such a list of commodities that are not required for life in the spirit as would reach the dimensions of a store's catalog."[14] (Had Benson written this today, he probably would have said 'the Net.')

There are numerous scriptures that speak of heavenly mansions, such as John 14:2, Enos 1:27, Ether 12:32, and D&C 59:2, 76:111, and 98:18.

However, all heavenly ownership (crowns, principalities, and so on) comes by individual merit; that is, 1) made possible by divine grace, 2) relegated to us as we are ready, and, 3) on condition that we magnify it.

Personal ownership excludes no one from the enjoyment of anything "owned" by anyone else. For example, mansions have no locks and everyone in the realm is welcome to enter. There are no "no trespassing" signs. Everyone is welcomed everywhere.

The owner ("patron" may be a better word) of an orchard welcomes all to partake of the fruit, yet the fruit is not diminished. It appears that "supply" is infinite, regardless of demand. The law of consecration seems to be lived to its fullest with no poor among them.

Years ago, Kenny Rogers sang a song entitled "Reuben James." The words include, "there's a better world awaitin' for the meek." There surely is, beyond our ability to fathom.

NOTES

1. Borgia, Anthony, *More About Life in the World Unseen*, 67.
2. Ibid., 141.
3. Borgia, *Life in the World Unseen*, 30.
4. Ibid., 22–3, 115, 145–52.
5. Ibid., 111.
6. Ibid., 126.
7. Borgia, *More About Life in the World Unseen*, 149.
8. Borgia, *Here and Hereafter*, 95.
9. Borgia, *Life in the World Unseen*, 120.
10. Borgia, *More About Life in the World Unseen*, 31.
11. Borgia, *Life in the World Unseen*, 10.
12. Ibid., 111.
13. Borgia, *Here and Hereafter*, 55.
14. Borgia, *More About Life in the World Unseen*, 68.

Chapter 21
How Does an NDE Affect the Rest of One's Mortal Life?

> "Taking a journey to heaven and back transformed my faith into knowledge and my hope into reality."
> — Mary C. Neal

Thus far, we have looked at what NDE experiences have taught us about the spirit world. But what about this world? Can an experience with the spirit world teach us new things about this life. Yes, many!

Perhaps the premier scientific study of the permanent affects of an NDE produced thus far was written by Dr. Kenneth Ring, a professor emeritus and founder of the International Association for Near-Death Studies (IANDS). His research indicates that most people who have experienced an NDE state that it was the most impactful event of their lives.[1]

If an NDE is that important, what changes does it induce? For one, many come back with little or no fear of dying.

Brent L. Top and his wife Wendy report:

> In contrast to those who have never approached death . . . the vast majority of those who have died and returned testify that, at least for those who have lived decent lives, death is not only sweet but is also a magnification and perpetuation of every good and wonderful

thing and the diminution and discontinuation of every uncivil and undesirable mortal element.[2]

"If that is what death is like," said one NDEer in Raymond Moody's *The Light Beyond*, "then I am not afraid to go at all."[3]

There are other positive effects as well, according to Dr. Moody: "Most of the NDEers that I have met are mentally healthier than before the experience."[4]

Many also report greater empathy towards others. Dr. Eben Alexander, after his NDE and physical recovery, was so changed in his regard for others and tenderness toward them that one of his co-workers jokingly asked him, "Are you Eben's twin brother, or what?"[5]

Another common characteristic from an NDE is a desire to "spread the word!" Said Dr. Ritchie, "ever since the experience, I have carried a terrific sense of urgency to share it with the lonely, discouraged and diseased people such as alcoholics, drug addicts, and the social outcast."[6]

It is not surprising then that many find their burdens of life easier to bear. Dr. Moody offered the example of a woman who faces a particularly challenging life, but because of her NDE now has an attitude of "luminous serenity."[7]

Most NDEers return with an amazing sense of peace. With that peace often comes increased spirituality. Dr. Moody said, "They (the patients he had interviewed) all reported that their religious beliefs were strengthened."[8]

Similarly, Dr. Mary C. Neal reported: "Taking a journey to heaven and back transformed my faith into knowledge and my hope into reality." She testified that she gained an absolute knowledge that, "God is real, that He has a plan for each of us, and that there really is life after death. . . ."[9]

This knowledge, she reported, changed the way she experiences life:

I know that every day really does matter and that I need to be about God's business every day. I also know that God loves all people deeply and unconditionally . . . even those people whom I may not like or agree with. It motivates me to try to see the beauty in them that God sees.[10]

Rachel's Experience

I believe that life's purposes are magnified with each blessing or trial we experience. Further, my mortal life was significantly affected by my NDE. I have selected the three greatest: 1) The temporary nature of mortality; 2) The ability of direct communication with Heavenly Father; and 3) Knowledge of life after death.

I have gained a deep respect or reverence for my time here upon the earth because of my NDE. I now pay particular attention to the limited time I have as a mortal being. An ever-loving Father is over all, and life spent in mortality is according to His will. I now better recognize how the purpose of my earthly life is a part of the plan of salvation. I am aware that death can come anytime, anywhere, with no permission, and how easily it is to pass through the veil. Yet, I feel blessed with the comfort and peace the Holy Ghost provides.

My NDE has also affected my mortal life in that I know direct communication with my eternal Father in Heaven is possible through Jesus Christ. I value the importance of feeling or sensing the meaning of what I am struggling to relay to my Father in Heaven, rather than the use of words to solely communicate. Gram's message was transferred to me spiritually through the Holy Ghost, making comprehension utterly clear. Her spirit 'spoke' to my spirit.

President Boyd K. Packer taught, 'The Holy Ghost speaks with a voice that you feel more than you hear.'[11] Since my NDE, I am more tuned into those feelings. President Packer quoted passages from the Book of Mormon to better explain, 'We are told that 'angels speak by the power of the Holy Ghost.'' We are even told that when we speak by the power of the Holy Ghost we 'speak with the tongues [or in the same language] of angels' (*2 Nephi 31:13; 2 Nephi 32:2*).

I strive daily to pray to my Heavenly Father in the name of Jesus Christ and plead for safety, comfort, and forgiveness. I pledge my complete devotion and obedience to the Father. When I recommit, my fears are replaced with courage, my concerns replaced with tranquility, and my downtrodden spirit is filled with hope. The love and acceptance the Almighty sends through the Holy Ghost is a sure witness of truth. President Joseph Fielding Smith taught, 'The Spirit of God speaking to the spirit of man has power to impart truth with greater effect and understanding than the truth can be imparted by personal contact even with heavenly beings.'[12]

Through sincere prayer I can receive personal revelation. I readily notice the ever-gentle prodding of the Holy Ghost in answer to my honest communication with the Divine. I recognize these familiar promptings as those I knew in the spirit world. Countless times I have been prompted to simply stop 'doing' and 'be still.'

It is during these times of stillness I can identify the power of the Holy Ghost as His spirit communes with mine, resulting in a renewed strength of the Lord's will. These thoughts are communicated in a few seconds but are piercingly clear. It is when I heed these whisperings of the Spirit that I receive aid in calming my worries and, at the same time, increasing my hopes.

'For behold, again I say unto you that if ye will enter in by the way, and receive the Holy Ghost, it will show unto you all things what ye should do' (*2 Nephi 21:5*). 'But the Comforter, which is the Holy Ghost, whom the Father will send in my name, he shall teach you all things, and bring all things to your remembrance, whatsoever I have said unto you' (*John 14:26*).

Personal revelation seems natural and familiar to the time spent in the spirit world. I feel grateful to my Heavenly Father for this pure, direct, and individual communication.

Along with the blessings of a greater respect for

mortality, knowledge of sincere prayer and personal revelation, I have also been blessed with knowing the empathy and concern my loved ones living on the other side have for me.

Realizing this truth not only intensifies my love for them but also causes me to be more conscious of them. I can more fully comprehend the complex reality of life after death and the association with the spirit world. Such is inherently simple. I have gained an enduring connection to the next life. Likewise, I now have an ongoing and expanding appreciation of those living beyond the veil who sincerely assist and guide me as I struggle through mortality. Heavenly assistants urge my spirit to obey and persevere. This awareness is much more than simply feeling the presence of spirits or personages: it is a certain knowledge that loved relatives and friends who have died indeed live, though I cannot see them. The Holy Ghost strongly testifies of the surety of the spirit world.

Combined, these three concepts have heightened my level of trust, strengthened my faith, and increased my testimony of Jesus Christ.

NOTES

1. Ring, Kenneth, *Heading Toward Omega*, 23.
2. Top, Brent L. and Wendy C., *Glimpses Beyond Death's Door*, 249.
3. Moody, Raymond, *The Light Beyond*, 38.
4. Ibid.
5. Alexander, Eben, *Proof of Heaven*, 200.
6. Ritchie, George G., *Ordered to Return*, 15.
7. Moody, *The Light Beyond*, 40.
8. Ibid., 131.
9. Neal, Mary C., *To Heaven and Back*, xii.
10. Ibid., 219.
11. Packer, Boyd K., "The Gift of the Holy Ghost: What Every Member Should Know," Address given at the Missionary Training Center, Provo, Utah, 2003.
12. Smith, Joseph Fielding, *Doctrines of Salvation*, Vol. II, 273.

Wesley M. White

Chapter 22
Transition to the Spirit World

> "There's almost like this built-in mechanism of serenity or safety, and the fear of death kind of diminishes . . . The predominant themes are of love and forgiveness."
> — *Christopher Kerr*

On July 10, 2018, the Ogden, Utah, *Standard Examiner* newspaper included an article by Gary Rotstein of the *Pittsburg Post-Gazette*. It is entitled "Near Death, Seeing Dead People May Be Neither Rare nor Eerie." Rotstein introduces us to Beth Roncevich, who tells of sitting with her mother at the side of the bed of her dying father. Her dying father unexpectedly laughed. She asked what he was laughing at. He said, "Oh, we're all together. Everybody's together and we're having a wonderful time. We're having so much fun."

Roncevich went on to become a hospice nurse. Rotstein subsequently interviewed her and reported that she, and others who work with the dying, speak of patients who have talked about a vision, dream, or hallucination concerning someone who preceded them in death.

> It is often a long-lost loved one—mothers are most common, but fathers, siblings, grandparents and even pets also frequently show up, seemingly welcoming to whatever lies next . . . It is always a calming experience

> ... Even in an unconscious state, their arms will lift up as though taking someone else's hand, and their mouths will move as though speaking to someone.

Rotstein also told of a research study by The Center for Hospice & Palliative Care, located in a suburb of Buffalo, New York. The CEO, Christopher Kerr, stated, "As we approach death, dreams increase dramatically in frequency, and the dreams increasing most frequently have to do with the deceased—the loved ones who have passed."

Kerr said of the study:

> Of participants in that study, more than half the time they were reported to be either awake or a combination of asleep and awake during their experiences. In about three-fifths of cases, there was a theme of preparing to go somewhere. In fewer than one of five instances, the patient reported distress from the dream or vision.
>
> There's almost like this built-in mechanism of serenity or safety, and the fear of death kind of diminishes ... The predominant themes are of love and forgiveness.

Dr. Kerr related that he had advised a nurse that a terminally ill patient still had quality time ahead if given IV antibiotics and other fluids. The nurse suggested otherwise. When Dr. Kerr asked why, the nurse replied, "Because he's seeing his deceased mother."

Rotstein related an experience of Katie Hayes, of the same hospice. "Katie recalled an elderly woman terminally ill with heart disease whom she got to know well over a period of months."

Katie reported:

> One day I went to her, and she was in bed. I sat down, and she said, 'Katie, you'll never believe what I saw last night. I saw all of my loved ones who have passed on before me. My mother, husband, sister—they were all standing right at the front of my bed.'
>
> I said, 'Wow, that is amazing,' and the next day she passed.

Transition to the Spirit World

Melissa Brestensky, a nurse at a different facility, said:

> I've seen patients sit there and have a conversation with someone I couldn't see. I had one particular patient—it was hours later she passed away—she was describing the angels in the hallway, saying, 'Look at how beautiful they are, they are in beautiful white gowns.'

Rotstein also wrote that a Mrs. Darin Martin told of her late husband's sightings before his death: "First, he saw his youngest brother, who had died in 1980, sitting on the couch." Mrs. Martin said that later, her husband made sure that she and his deceased brother stepped out of the way of their deceased Great Dane, Czar. She concluded, "I truly believe when you die and go to heaven you have family and friends there to meet you."

Maria DePasquale, a hospice nurse for over 38 years, explains how she typically responds to a terminally ill person who reports seeing deceased loved ones and associates: "I maybe ask, 'Well, what do you think they're doing there?' They say something like, 'I think they're telling me it's time, it's time.' Then I say, 'Well, isn't it nice that somebody's there to share that with you.'"[1]

It is very common for NDEers to report meeting and associating with deceased friends and relatives. Some people, as they are beginning to transition to the spirit world, speak of deceased loved ones as if they were present. Many reach out as if being received by someone. Brigham Young, just before he passed on, exclaimed "Joseph!" three times.[2]

When I was a young boy, my widowed and elderly maternal grandmother lived with us for several years. She was wonderful, with many godly attributes. I remember threading needles for her as she did our mending. When she was near death, my mother, her sister, and I were with her in her bedroom. Suddenly my mother and aunt turned to each other and said, almost in unison, "Dad is here."

I admit that within seconds I had run well down the hall, but I soon heard my mother say, "She's gone." I returned to the bedroom and felt the sacred spirit associated with the passing. An initially frightening experience had become my first witness of the reality of the spirit world and of continuing relationships.

Again, we turn to Robert Hugh Benson for additional detail:

> To leave the earth world and to take up permanent residence in the spirit world is not such a personal upheaval as some people might be disposed to imagine ... When we pass into the spirit world, we meet again those of our relatives and friends who have passed over before us ... The meetings with relations and friends are something that must be experienced in order to grasp the full significance and joy of reunion. These gatherings will continue for some while after the arrival of the new resident. It is natural that in the novelty both of surroundings and condition some time should be spent in a grand exchange of news, and in hearing of all that has transpired in the spirit lives of those who have 'predeceased' us. Eventually the time will come when the newly-arrived individual will begin to consider what he is to do with his spirit life.[3]

To provide you more insights into this transition that awaits all of us, I include a few separate vignettes from the book *At the Hour of Death* by Karlis Osis and Erlendur Haraldsson, PhDs:

- All of a sudden she opened her eyes. She called her [deceased] husband by name and said she was coming to him. She had the most peaceful, nicest smile just as though she were going to the arms of someone she thought a great deal of. She said, 'Guy, I am coming.' She didn't seem to realize I was there. It was almost as if she were in another world. It was as if something beautiful had opened up to her; she was experiencing something so wonderful and beautiful.[4]

- Suddenly she looked eagerly towards one part of the room, a radiant smile illuminating her whole countenance. 'Oh, lovely, lovely,' she said. I asked, 'What is lovely?' 'What I see,' she said in low, intense tones. 'What do you see?' 'Lovely brightness—wonderful beings.' It is difficult to describe the sense of reality conveyed by her intense absorption in the vision. Then—seeming to focus her attention more intently on one place for a moment—she exclaimed, almost with a kind of joyous cry, 'Why, it's Father? Oh, he's so glad I'm coming; he is so glad. It would be perfect if only W. (her husband) would come too.'[5]

- Deathbed patients see apparitions more often when fully conscious and having proper awareness and capability of responding to the environment than when awareness and communication are impaired[6]... In a very soft voice, and with a smile on her face, she had an endearing conversation about how much she loved him [her husband], how much she missed him, and how she knew she would join him. She said, 'It won't be long now before I'll be with you.' Reaching out as if she felt [her husband's] hand, she said 'You look well cared for.'[7]

- Her consciousness was also very, very clear—no sedation, no hallucinogenic history. She was cheerful and confident that she would recover and return to her daughter who badly needed her at home. Suddenly she stretched out her arms and, smiling, called to me. 'Can't you see Charlie [her dead husband] there with outstretched arms? I'm wondering why I haven't gone home before.' Describing the vision she said, 'What a beautiful place with all the flowers and music. Don't you hear it? Oh, girls, don't you see Charlie?' She said he was waiting for her. I feel she definitely saw her husband.[8]

- A Hindu farmer in his fortieth year was suffering from liver disease. He told [his doctor] he felt himself flying through the air and into another world where he saw gods sitting and calling him. He thought he was going to meet those gods; he wanted to be there, saying to those around him, 'Let me go.' Relatives tried to talk him out of it telling him he would be O.K. He should not go. But the patient was very happy to see those gods and he was ready to die. He went into a deep coma a short time later,

and died in two days. He was clear and coherent while describing what he 'saw.'[9]
- A 68–year-old Polish housewife was afflicted with cancer. Her mind was clear. She was settling some financial matters and asked for her purse. She had not thought of dying. Then she saw her husband who had died twenty years before. She was happy, with a sort of religious feeling, and according to her doctor, she lost all fear of death. Instead of fearing death, she felt it to be the logical, correct thing. She died within 5 or 10 minutes.[10]

These experiences sit well with comments by President James E. Faust in his eighty-third year: "As we get older, the pull from our parents and grandparents on the other side of the veil becomes stronger. It is a sweet experience when they visit us in our dreams."[11] Emma Smith's last words were "Joseph! Yes, yes, I'm coming."[12]

The Other Side of the Veil

The above observations, of course, come from this side of the veil. The "view" from the other side is also noteworthy.

We begin with Benson explaining the 'attachment' of the body to the spirit:

> The spirit body exactly coincides with the physical body... The former is attached to the latter by a magnetic cord. I call it a magnetic cord for lack of a better name [remember the 'snow' principle mentioned in Chapter 10]. So long as the magnetic cord is joined to the earthly body, just so long will earthly life remain in the physical body. But the moment that dissolution takes place the lifeline is severed, the spirit is free to live in its own element, while the body will decay in the manner which is perfectly familiar to you upon earth.[13]

Benson further explained that separation:

> ... wherein the spirit body becomes gradually and easily detached from the earthly body in a slow and steady process of separation. The magnetic cord, in such

cases, will detach from the earthly [body] gently; it will fall away naturally, just as the leaf falls from the tree in the autumn. When the leaf is in full life and vigor it requires a strong action to dislodge it from the tree. And so it is with the spirit body. In the young, the cohesion is firm, but it gradually lessens as age increases.[14]

What about "atypical" death? Benson provided this example:

It is when we come to transitions where the physical body is literally disintegrated, blown into fragments in a second of time, that the greatest distress and discomfort are caused to the spirit body. The magnetic cord is snapped off, or wrenched away, almost as though the limb of the physical body were torn from the socket. The spirit body finds itself suddenly dispossessed of its earthly tenement, but not before the physical shock of disintegration has been transmitted to the spirit body.

Not only is there extreme bewilderment, but the shock has something of a paralyzing effect. The [spirit] person so situated may be incapable of movement for the time being. In many instances sleep will intervene. He will remain in the place of his dissolution, but we come to his rescue, and carry him away to one of the rest homes specially provided for such cases.

Here he will receive treatment from experts, and ultimately the patient will recover his full health beyond any shadow of doubt. The cure is certain and complete. There is no such thing as a relapse or recurrence of the indisposition. Perhaps the most difficult part of the treatment comes when a full consciousness is restored, and the patient begins to ask questions![15]

Concerning the nature of the spirit after transition to the spirit world, Benson expressed:

A person is exactly the same the moment after he has 'died' as he was the moment before. No magical, instantaneous change takes place either of mind or [spirit] body. We pass into the spirit world with all our earthly likes and dislikes, all our fancies and foibles, all our idiosyncrasies, and with all our religious errors fast upon us.[16]

Sound familiar? In the Book of Mormon, Amulek expressed it thusly to the Zoramites: "That same spirit which doth possess your bodies at the time that ye go out of this life, that same spirit will have power to possess your body in that eternal world" (*Alma 34:34*).

Monsignor Benson clarified what he (and Amulek) taught: "We are just as we were on earth, though it does not follow in every instance that we will behave just as we did on earth."[17]

However, the ambiance of the spirit world soon impacts our behavior.

Benson explained:

> The beauties and charms of these realms act like an intellectual tonic; they bring out only that which is and always was the very best in one. Whatever was not the very best in one upon earth will be swamped by the good nature and kindness which the very air here will bring out, like some choice bloom beneath the warm summer sun . . . We are no longer subject to the stress that produces the unpleasant qualities that were observable in us when we were on the earth. Remove the causes of the distempers and the latter will disappear also.[18]

I take this to mean that this change to a much more pleasant environment facilitates advancement for those who desire to improve.

However, because most mortals scarcely ponder our next life, and religious creeds (plus Hollywood movies and our celebrations of Halloween) generally offer a very distorted view of the next world, most of the deceased "arrive in a state of bewilderment and complete ignorance of the fact that they have passed from the earth world."[19]

"The rest for the newly-arrived person is frequently advisable, or necessary," expressed Benson, "to allow for adjustment of the spirit body to its new conditions of life."[20]

Chapter 11 provides additional details concerning these "halls of rest." I believe this "rest" spoken of by Benson is a part of the "rest" promised by the Savior (see *Matthew 11:28*).

To reaffirm Rachel's experience from Chapter 12:

Rachel's Experience

When my earthly time is complete and it is time to enter the spirit world, which is the next phase of the Lord's plan, I know I will not fear . . . I will at last be able to see the faces of my beloved heavenly friends and relatives, and any fear will be replaced with complete peace.

NOTES

1. Rotstein, Gary, "Near Death, Seeing Dead People May Be Neither Rare nor Eerie," *Pittsburg Post-Gazette*, various.
2. Arrington, Leonard J., *Brigham Young, American Moses*, 399.
3. Borgia, Anthony, *Life in the World Unseen*, 170.
4. Osis, Karlis and Haraldsson, Erlendur, *At the Hour of Death*, 4.
5. Ibid., 16-17.
6. Ibid., 32.
7. Ibid., 42.
8. Ibid., 83.
9. Ibid., 105.
10. Ibid., 113.
11. Faust, James E., "Dear Are the Sheep That Have Wandered." General Conference, April 2003.
12. Quoted in the *Encyclopedia of Latter-day Saint History* by Donald Q. Cannon, 1113.
13. Borgia, *Here and Hereafter*, 15–16.
14. Ibid., 47.
15. Ibid., 48.
16. Ibid., 39.
17. Ibid.
18. Ibid., 124–5.
19. Ibid., 21.
20. Ibid., 45.

Wesley M. White

Chapter 23
Divine Light and Love

> "These beings aren't composed of ordinary light. They glow with a beautiful and intense luminescence that seems to permeate everything and fill the person with love."
> — *Raymond Moody*

If this book had to be condensed into just a few words, I would choose "The Light and Love of God for His Children." Some NDErs are privileged to enjoy a powerful, personal, intimate expression of this love. Dr. Raymond Moody describes the process:

> Many NDEers enjoy an experience with a personage of light. In most cases, they express that the brilliance of the light is indescribable, yet does not dazzle or hurt the eyes, nor keep them from seeing other objects. Almost unanimously, they express that it is a being of light that communicates with them.
>
> Some attribute human features to this being, and some do not. In all cases, the NDEer feels an irresistible attraction to this being of light.
>
> It is a personal being. It has a very definite personality. The love and warmth which emanate from this being are utterly beyond words, and he feels completely surrounded by it and taken up in it, completely at ease and accepted in the presence of this being.[1]

He further explains:

> These beings aren't composed of ordinary light. They glow with a beautiful and intense luminescence that seems to permeate everything and fill the person with love. In fact, one person who went through this experience said, 'I could describe this as light or [as] love and it would mean the same thing.' Some say that it's almost like being drenched by a rainstorm of light. They also describe the light as being much brighter than anything we experience on earth. But still, despite its brilliant intensity, it doesn't hurt the eyes. Instead, it's warm, vibrant, and alive.[2]

Sometimes the NDEer associates this being with someone they revere in their religion, such as Jesus Christ,[3] but most do not. Perhaps it is an ancestor who has reached such a stage of glory. Dr. Moody reported, "Some have said that it's neither God nor Jesus, but someone very holy nonetheless."[4]

In fact, Dr. Ritchie, upon visiting the highest realm, stated that "the inhabitants [there] exuded light almost as brilliant as the Christ."[5]

It is frequently this being of light who conducts a personal review of one's mortality:

> Generally, the NDEer experiences a life review (although it is not universal to all NDEs). As a prelude to the review, the glorious being asks a question such as 'What have you done with your life to show me?' or, 'What have you done with your life that is sufficient?' . . . Incidentally, all insist that this question, ultimate and profound as it may be in its emotional impact, is not at all asked in condemnation. This being, all seem to agree, does not direct the question to accuse or to threaten, for they still feel the total love and acceptance coming from the light, no matter what their answer may be. Rather, the point of the question seems to be to make them think about their lives, to draw them out.[6]

To me, these questions seem to be a very appropriate way to begin the next life. It's like measuring where on the spectrum of progress one finds himself and sets the tone for progress in the next phase of eternal life.

My wife experienced a preview of this sacred interview. She was in a temple waiting to do a session. It had been a harried, frustrating, and challenging day. When looking at a painting of the Second Coming showing the Savior with outstretched arms, how she wished she could embrace Him. A voice came into her mind and expressed, "That day will come, and the first thing I will ask you is, 'Who have you brought with you?'"

We culminate this study with first-hand experiences of some NDErs who enjoyed sacred personage-of-light experiences.

- It was a total immersion in light, brightness, warmth, peace, security.[7]
- There was the warmest, most wonderful love. Love all around me . . . I felt light-good-happy-joy-at ease. Forever—eternal love.[8]
- The light communicates to you and for the first time in your life . . . is a feeling of true, pure love. It can't be compared to the love of your wife, the love of your children. . . All of these wonderful, wonderful feelings combined could not possibly compare to the feeling, the true love.[9]
- Love is, without a doubt, the basis of everything. Not some abstract, hard-to-fathom kind of love but the day-to-day kind that everyone knows—the kind of love we feel when we look at our spouse and our children, or even our animals. In its purest and most powerful form, this love is not jealous or selfish, but unconditional. This is the reality of realities, the incomprehensibly glorious truth of truths that lives and breathes at the core of everything that exists or that will ever exist.[10]
- And this enormously bright light seemed almost to cradle me. I just seemed to exist in it and be part of it and

be nurtured by it, and the feeling just became more and more and more ecstatic and glorious and perfect. And everything about it was—if you took the one thousand best things that ever happened to you in your life and multiplied them by a million, maybe you could get close to this feeling.[11]

This same NDEer further states:

- I have never, before or since, seen anything as beautiful, loving, and perfectly pleasant as this being. An immense, radiant love poured from it. An incredible light shone through every single pore of its face. The colors of the light were magnificent, vibrant, and alive. The light radiated outward. It was a brilliant white superimposed with what I can only describe as a golden hue. I was filled with an intense feeling of joy and awe.[12]
- I knew that [the light] was omnipotent, that it represented infinite divine love . . . Even though the light seemed thousands and thousands of times stronger than the brightest sunlight, it did not bother my eyes.[13]
- By my side was a Being with a magnificent presence. I could not see an exact form, but instead, a radiation of light that lit up everything about me and spoke with a voice that held the deepest tenderness one can ever imagine . . . as this loving yet powerful Being spoke to me, I understood vast meanings, much beyond my ability to explain.[14]

A Testimony

I'm not anxious to leave this life anytime soon, but thanks to the plan of salvation, I do know that I don't fear the prospect. All the things I've learned about the spirit world give me not only a sense of peace but also a bit of longing to experience the marvels that apparently await us there. After a life that may be filled with more than a few physical trials and challenges, who wouldn't want to go to a place where they will never again experience pain, illness, injury, or the possibility of dying? I also long to see my loved ones who have already passed through the veil, and I look forward with excitement to soaking up all the knowledge in the universe.

An acquaintance recently said one thing she is most looking forward to is meeting all the people she has admired from history. She'd love to have a chat with Moses and Abraham, or Joseph Smith and Nephi. She said someone told her, "You really think you'll get to meet those important people? Forget about it." She wanted to reply, "You bet I will! Want to know why? Because people like you won't be in line ahead of me. You'll all be standing on the sidelines watching while I'm meeting my heroes and saying things like, '"Captain Moroni! I'm such a fan!'"

As great as it would be to meet the luminaries, what about those who were never famous but had led fascinating lives? What about chatting with a woman who was in the crowd of thousands when Jesus visited the Nephites? Maybe she was also a granddaughter of one of the 2,000 stripling warriors. Or talking with a young girl who was on the hillside when the Savior gave the Sermon on the Mount or when He miraculously fed the multitude. Since time is different there, perhaps we'd have the opportunity to talk with millions of people who have shared this earth with us but at different times and places.

And besides greeting our departed friends and family or people from history, what a thrill it will be to see our Savior Jesus Christ again! Former Apostle Melvin J. Ballard, while on his mission as a young man, prayed to know if he was doing the Lord's will. In confirmation, he had a dream in which he found himself entering a room in the temple:

> 'As I entered the door,' Elder Ballard said, 'I saw, seated on a raised platform, the most glorious Being my eyes have ever beheld or that I ever conceived existed in all

the eternal worlds. As I approached to be introduced, he arose and stepped towards me with extended arms, and he smiled as he softly spoke my name. If I shall live to be a million years old, I shall never forget that smile. He took me into his arms and kissed me, pressed me to his bosom, and blessed me, until the marrow of my bones seemed to melt! When he had finished, I fell at his feet, and, as I bathed them with my tears and kisses, I saw the prints of the nails in the feet of the Redeemer of the world. The feeling that I had in the presence of him who hath all things in his hands, to have his love, his affection, and his blessing was such that if I ever can receive that of which I had but a foretaste, I would give all that I am, all that I ever hope to be, to feel what I then felt!"[15]

I'm sure I'm not alone when I say I greatly anticipate receiving that bone-melting hug for myself.

In summary, because of Christ, our progress—and that of our loved ones—can be forever. God be praised!

NOTES

1. Moody, Raymond, *Life after Life*, 43.
2. Moody, *The Light Beyond*, 12.
3. Moody, *Life after Life*, 46.
4. Moody, *The Light Beyond*, 13.
5. Ritchie, George, G., *Ordered to Return*, 45.
6. Moody, *Life After Life*, 45.
7. Ring, Kenneth, *Headed Toward Omega*, 53.
8. Ibid., 55.
9. Ibid., 58.
10. Alexander, Eben, *Proof of Heaven*, 112.
11. Ring, 62.
12. Ibid., 65.
13. Ibid., 66.
14. Ibid., 75.
15. Quoted by Bryant S. Hinckley, in *Sermons and Missionary Service of Melvin J. Ballard*, 156.

Chapter 24
The Divine Role of Jesus Christ in Our Next Life

> "The Atonement will not only help us overcome our transgressions and mistakes, but in His time, it will resolve all inequities of life—those things that are unfair which are the consequences of circumstances or others' acts and not our own decisions."
> — *Elder Richard G. Scott*

One of the most difficult questions for those who struggle with belief in God is: *Why did God, if He is all loving and all powerful, create a world in which there is so much injustice, so much suffering, and so much evil?*

Also, *Why does He allow plagues, earthquakes, floods, and other disasters that snuff out the life of so many innocent people? Why does He allow evil people to abuse good people? Why would a compassionate God allow a young father with a wife and small children who depend upon him to die? Why would he take my child, an innocent little boy whom I loved so much, upon whom so much of my life's meaning and happiness were centered?*

Failure to find acceptable answers to these questions has led many to abandon their belief in God. *This is heartbreaking, as there are answers!*

The answers are found in our Heavenly Father's plan of salvation, which would not exist without His Son. So this last chapter is devoted to our Savior's role in the next stage of our progression.

God the Father's Eternal Mission

Often neglected in the writings of well-meaning theologians, is the incomprehensible and unconditional love God, our Heavenly Father, has for His children. That love is the motivation for all that is real—the creation, the universe, our earthly experience, and our eventual life in the hereafter.

Because of that love, God has one objective, and one objective only—to get His children back.[1] "For behold, this is my work and my glory—to bring to pass the immortality and eternal life of man" (*Moses 1:39*). It is my belief that an all-knowing and all-loving God will bless all His children's efforts to reach that objective.

"Those who put themselves in his hands," wrote author and scholar C. S. Lewis, "will become perfect—perfect in love, wisdom, joy, beauty, and immortality. The change *will not* be completed in this life, *for death is an important part of the treatment.*"[2] (Italics added).

Jesus Christ, the Son of God, became our Savior by perfectly carrying out the plan and will of His Father. He paid the price for our sins, our suffering, and the sting of Death. This was His great Atonement, and it is still available to help us repent and improve in the next life!

As we come to better understand the great gift of the Atonement in this life as well as in our next life, we will come to realize the glorious truth—no one is counted out.

Jesus Christ's Great Earthly Ministry

During His great ministry, Jesus Christ healed the sick, caused the blind to see, miraculously provided food, and even raised the dead. He exponentially reduced the suffering (and thereby improved the mortal life) of many people. The New Testament documents 34 miracles,[3] and John clarifies that there were countless more (*John 21:25*). However, Christ's mortal mission encompassed only three years—limiting His dealings to a narrow swath of the infirmities of the world.

Philip Yancey, author of *The Jesus I Never Knew*, expressed it this way, "Jesus, with a few dozen healings, did little to solve the problem of pain on this planet. He did, however, give the World a glimpse of how things really should be, and are, except in a fallen world."

Yancey further taught that death, decay, entropy, and destruction are not God's laws, but rather the suspensions of God's laws for the time of our mortality. His miracles provided us a glimpse of the state of the righteous in the next life.[4]

It is not entirely known how the tragedies of this world can endow us with the personal characteristics and attributes necessary to know full joy in the presence of our Heavenly Father. The Apostle Paul declared that "all things work together for good for them that love God" (*Romans 8:28*). We also know that many of these experiences can teach compassion, humility, and faith. Perhaps in the next world, we will kneel at Our Savior's feet to express appreciation for all the experiences we felt were so terrible in this life —ones that in an eternal perspective provide the means for eternal life and joy. Those events we view as hardships and tragedies in this life may in the next be recognized as blessings.

His Greater Message

Jesus' great ministry included His even greater message, which revealed what we must do to be more like Him and the Father. In His Sermon on the Mount, He introduced tough standards! "Whosoever shall smite thee on thy right cheek, turn to him the other also . . . if any man will . . . take away thy coat, let him have thy cloak also . . . Love your enemies . . . do good to them that hate you, and pray for them which despitefully use you" (*Matthew 5:39-40, 44*).

C. S. Lewis commented on this command in these words:

> Some people seem to think that means 'unless you are perfect, I will not help you'. . . . He meant 'The only help I will give you is help to become perfect. You may want something less; but I will give you nothing less.'

He continues by paraphrasing the Savior:

> I will never rest, nor let you rest, until you are literally perfect—until my Father can say without reservation that He is well pleased with you, as He said he was pleased with me' . . . and yet—this is the other and equally important side to it—this Helper who will, in the long run, be satisfied with nothing less than absolute perfection, will also be delighted with the first feeble, stumbling efforts you make today and tomorrow.[5]

Christian writer George MacDonald, who was influential in Lewis' conversion to Christianity, declared, "God is easy to please, but hard to satisfy."[6] Through Gethsemane and the crucifixion, in atoning for the sins of man, Christ made it possible for us to be made pure—and capable of experiencing eternal joy in His presence.

The most important part of the Savior's mission, referred to as the Atonement, can be divided into two parts, which overlapped: His emotional and spiritual suffering, and His physical suffering.

His Greatest Gift

In his extraordinary book, *The Infinite Atonement*, Elder Tad R. Callister (a General Authority of the Church) remarked, "It seems we tend to concentrate on the first two categories [His earthly ministry and His message], while His mission, the redemption of the world [and of the next world] supersedes all else in the history of the universe."[7] Without His mission, called the Atonement of Jesus Christ: 1) we could have no forgiveness of any of our sins, ever; 2) we could make no progress in this life, the next, or forever; 3) and all hope for mankind would be gone (as well as additional consequences (*Alma, chapters 40 and 41*).

This central event in the universe merits examination. Most of the first part took place in the Garden of Gethsemane. Little is provided by the scriptures of His experience there for two reasons. First, it was very sacred, and, like the Transfiguration, cannot be detailed while maintaining its sacredness.

Second, there were no witnesses. Even though Peter, James, and John—His three primary apostles—went to the Garden with Him, they slept a stone's cast away from Him.

From the scriptures, we do know that as the event approached, He began to be sorrowful and heavy. "And He went a little further, and fell on His face, and prayed, saying, O my Father, if it be possible, let this cup pass from me" (*Matthew 26: 38-39*).

Mark tells us that He "began to be sore amazed, and to be very heavy" (*Mark 14: 33*). Luke, who essentially wrote his gospel on behalf of Peter, tells us, "And being in agony he prayed more earnestly: and his sweat was as it were great drops of blood falling down to the ground" (*Luke 22:44*).

While traditional Christianity focuses on the physical suffering of the crucifixion, modern-day revelation divulges that Jesus lamented the emotional and spiritual suffering in Gethsemane even more (*D&C 19:18*).

Wrote Elder Neal A. Maxwell (of the Quorum of the Twelve Apostles): "The cumulative weight of all mortal sins, somehow, past, present, and future, pressed upon that perfect, sinless, and sensitive soul! All infirmities and sicknesses were part, too, of the awful arithmetic of the Atonement."[8]

At another time, Elder Maxwell taught: "He bore our sins to atone for them and our sicknesses to understand them."[9]

Why was it such an important part of His mission? What did it accomplish?

Wrote Apostle Richard G. Scott: "The Atonement will not only help us overcome our transgressions and mistakes, but in His time, it will resolve all inequities of life—those things that are unfair which are the consequences of circumstances or others' acts and not our own decisions."[10]

Elder Gerritt W. Gong, of the Quorum of the Twelve Apostles, expressed it concisely when he said, "[Christ] came to pay a debt He didn't owe because we owed a debt we couldn't pay."[11]

A Remarkable Testimony of Gethsemane

Some years ago, a dear and trusted friend who strives full-heartedly to follow the Savior shared with me a sacred experience which enlightened him on what occurred in Gethsemane. He graciously permitted me to include it in this book:

> While serving as a missionary for the Lord Jesus Christ, I had a marvelous experience. On May 20th, 2001, I was having an especially difficult day. I had suffered months of persecution by some who were supposed to be my friends and brothers in the Lord. I was feeling low about myself and my self-worth. I remember feeling 'am I worthy to serve in the name of the Lord?' I was really struggling with self-doubt. That night I felt as if I was in the depths of hell, and my heart was very troubled. In my personal prayers, I asked my Heavenly Father if He was pleased with me. Then I asked Him if I had been forgiven of my sins.
>
> I stayed on my knees for quite some time. I felt calm and at peace during that time, but I didn't feel that my prayer was answered. I didn't get a piercing feeling, and my bosom didn't burn. My desire was so strong to receive an answer that I stayed on my knees longer, but it

still felt like I did not get an answer. Feeling my fatigue from the long, hard day, I decided that I would try again the next day, and I toppled into bed.

While I was lying there, my heart stirred within me: I was [still] genuinely concerned that I wasn't right before the Lord. My anxiety finally got the best of me. I decided to get out of bed and pray again. As I knelt down, my tears began to flow freely. My heart was pained, and I began pleading before God. I begged, I mean I really begged with all that I had in me, for mercy. I expressed my absolute love and devotion for my Father in Heaven.

While I was pouring out my soul to Him, a vision opened up before me. I saw the Savior of the World in the Garden of Gethsemane. He was on His hands and knees, in great agony and pain, beyond description. His clothes were stained red, and His hair was wet and clumped with His precious blood. I saw His face twisted with pain. I saw His hand scratching the bark of an olive tree, as he bled great drops of blood from every pore. My heart wrenched for Him, and I knew He was paying for my sins, my pride, my selfishness. The Son of God, the Perfect and Holy Man that had done no wrong, was taking my sins, my mistakes, my evil, my darkness, and was paying the price in my behalf.

The vision was very quick, opening and closing within a few seconds. A voice then came into my head and told me to be obedient. I have never been the same person since seeing the Savior of the world suffer personally for me. Words cannot describe my feelings for the Son of God. I absolutely love Him.[12]

My friend's experience leads well into Paul's experience on the road to Damascus, where he (as Saul) intended to continue his persecution of Christians. The Savior appeared to him and said, "Saul, Saul, why persecutest thou me?" (*Acts 26:14*). It is fully appropriate that the Savior should say to Paul "me" rather than "the church" or "the saints," because He personally had also suffered the pains of those who Paul had persecuted.

The Savior had the power to forgive Paul's sins. Through the Atonement, Christ had already paid the price and had, therefore, satisfied justice for all of Paul's wicked deeds—including the suffering Paul had inflicted upon others.

Paul subsequently did his part to repent by completely changing his ways (and his name), courageously testifying of Christ, serving His cause, suffering imprisonment and torture, and dying as a martyr. Paul corrected the results of his sins the best he could. The Savior did the rest. Paul's example of repentance provides an example for all of us who love the Lord.

C. S. Lewis wrote, "It apparently costs God nothing, so far as we know, to create nice things, but to convert rebellious wills cost Him crucifixion."[13] Because of His universal sacrifice, we can receive salvation instead of what we deserve. As Yancey expresses it, "[The Atonement] breaks the logjam between justice and forgiveness."[14]

So, Christ paid the price of all human sin and suffering, past, present, and future. Now all mankind can be forgiven from its sins, though not while *in* its sins.

I don't pretend to understand the "math" of the Atonement, but as Lewis said, "A man can eat his dinner without understanding exactly how food nourishes him. A man can accept what Christ has done without knowing how it works."[15]

Because we are all familiar with the tremendous suffering associated with the second phase of the Atonement, which began later that same night with Christ's arrest, we will not detail it here, but simply remind ourselves of the result, remembering the sacred declaration of angels at the empty tomb: "He is not here: for He is risen" (*Matthew 28:6*). His resurrection is the crowning event of all history. Christ overcame death, and therefore we will all live again. We learned more about the next life (where the Savior reigns) throughout this book.

Philip Yancey masterfully summarizes what we have discussed, " . . . God loves [us] because of who He is, not because of who we are."[16]

I add my view to Yancey's comment: God not only loves us because of who He is, but because of who we may become—an immense potential that can be realized, in this life and the next, only because of the Savior's atoning sacrifice. Blessed be His name!

NOTES

1. Ritchie, George, *Ordered to Return*, 170.
2. Lewis, C. S., *Mere Christianity*, 158.
3. Yancey, Philip, *The Jesus I Never Knew*, 14.
4. Ibid., 182.
5. Ibid., 183.
6. Lewis, Quoted in *Mere Christianity*, 58.
7. Callister, Tad, *The Infinite Atonement*, 5.
8. Maxwell, Neal L., "Yet Thou Art There," General Conference, October 1987.
9. Maxwell, *But for a Small Moment*, 92.
10. Scott, Richard G., "Jesus Christ, Our Redeemer," General Conference (of the Church of Jesus Christ of Latter-day Saints), April 1977.
11. Gong, Gerrit W., "Hosanna and Hallelujah—The Living Christ: The Heart of Restoration and Easter," General Conference, April 2020.
12. Document in author's possession.
13. Lewis, 165.
14. Yancey, Philip, *What's So Amazing About Grace?*, 82.
15. Lewis, 44.
16. Yancey, 82.

Wesley M. White

Author Biography

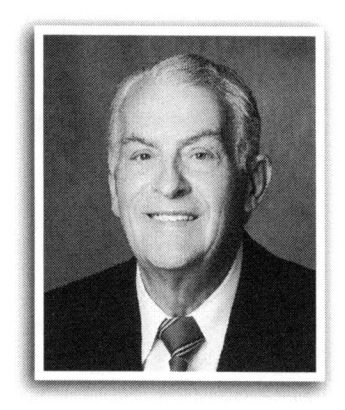

Wesley White proudly wore the uniform of the US Air Force for 36 years: as an ROTC cadet, command pilot, and JrROTC professor.

He has served seven years as a full-time missionary: as a young man in Texas, as president of the Florida Orlando Mission, and as director of the Mesa Temple Visitors' Center. He served as a stake president and currently serves as a temple sealer.

He earned a BA degree from BYU and an MPA from the University of Oklahoma.

He and his wife Kay have six living children, 22 grandchildren, and five great-grandchildren.

Acknowledgements

I am particularly indebted to my friend Richard McDermott, PhD, who vigorously encouraged me in my efforts.

He meticulously edited this book and has enhanced its flow, readability, and clarity. He recommended (and in some instances provided) resources that have proven vital to the unique perspective that sets this book apart from all other books pertaining to the next life. This is a much better book because of him.

Richard is a former university professor and author of two popular textbooks. He and his wife Carol have five children and 17 grandchildren.

I am also indebted to our amazing editor, Mary Mintz. Richard and I have worked with several editors—he has written two textbooks, and I've done a research book—but none even compared with Mary! As two examples (of hundreds I could list), she designed our wonderful cover, front and back, and suggested a much better title than the one we proposed. We use adjectives such as "marvelous" and "insightful" every time we speak of her work. Contact her at mary_mintz@yahoo.com, and she can help you get your book ready for publication, too.

WORKS CITED

Alexander, Eben. *Proof of Heaven*. New York: Simon and Schuster, 2012.

Arrington, Leonard J. *Brigham Young, American Moses*. New York: Random House.

"Articles of Faith" #13, *The Pearl of Great Price*. The Church of Jesus Christ of Latter-day Saints, 1880.

Benson, Ezra Taft. "Christ, Gifts and Expectations." Ensign Magazine, Dec. 1988.

——. "To the Children of the Church." General Conference of The Church of Jesus Christ of Latter-day Saints, Apr. 1989. *(In all future references, "General Conference" refers to the twice-yearly conference of the Church.)*

Benson, Robert Hugh. *Confessions of a Convert*. London: Longmans, Green and Co., 1913. One of the many books and plays that Benson wrote, including Life in the World Unseen (listed under Anthony Borgia). I read it to verify the same writing style as the books he dictated to Borgia. It was unquestionably the same. Benson was the son of Edward White Benson, the Archbishop of Canterbury. Robert followed in his father's ecclesiastical footsteps and became an Anglican priest, with the title of Monsignor. As he studied and began writing—he authored thirty-six books (thirteen of a religious nature) and several plays—he became uneasy in his own doctrinal position. The Church of England claimed no ecclesiastical authority, while the Catholic church claimed authority traced back to St. Peter. He converted to Roman Catholicism and became a chamberlain to the pope.

The Book of Mormon, The Church of Jesus Christ of Latter-day Saints, 1830.

Borgia, Anthony. *Heaven and Earth*. London: 7, 1995. Borgia was Benson's amanuensis for the four of the books that bear his name. In some, he is listed as if he were the author, and in others as "recorder."

——. *Here and Hereafter*. London: Psychic Press, 1968.

——. *Life in the World Unseen*. Midway, UT: M.A.P., 1993.

——. *More About Life in the World Unseen*. Midway, UT: M.A.P., 2000.

Burpo, Todd, with Vincent, Lynn. *Heaven Is for Real*. Nashville: Thomas Nelson, 2010. A cute book (and also a movie) about the NDE of a four-year-old boy, told in the purity and sincerity of a child. His father, a Christian minister, learns simple truths from his son's NDE that are in conflict with his theological training.

Callister, Tad R. *The Infinite Atonement*. Salt Lake City, UT: Deseret, 2000.

Crowther, Duane S. *Life Everlasting: A Definitive Study of Life After Death*. Bountiful, UT: Horizon, 1967.

Doctrine and Covenants Student Manual. Salt Lake City: Church Education System, 1981.

Eadie, Betty J. *Embraced by the Light*. New York: Bantam Books, 1992.

Cannon, Donald Q., *Encyclopedia of Latter-day Saint History*. Deseret Book, 2011.

Faust, James E. "The Atonement: Our Greatest Hope." General Conference, Oct. 2001.

——. "Dear Are the Sheep That Have Wandered." General Conference, Apr. 2003.

——. "A Royal Priesthood." General Conference, Apr. 2006.

——. "The Voice of the Spirit." Ensign Magazine, Jun. 2006.

——. "Woman, Why Weepest Thou?" General Conference, Oct.1996.

Gong, Gerritt W. "Hosanna and Hallelujah—The Living Christ: The Heart of the Restoration and Easter." General Conference, Apr. 2020.

Haraldsson, Erlendur, PhD, and Osis, Karlis, PhD. *At the Hour of Death*. Norwalk, CT: Hastings House, 1997.

Harnsberger, Caroline Thomas (compiler). Mark Twain at Your Fingertips: A Book of Quotations, p. 110.

Hill, Mary V. *Angel Children*. Bountiful, UT: Horizon, 1973.

Hinckley, Gordon B. "Faith in Every Footstep: The Epic Pioneer Journey." General Conference, Apr. 1997.

Holland, Jeffrey R. "The Ministry of Angels." General Conference, Oct. 2008.

Hunter, Howard W. "The Temptations of Christ." General Conference, Oct. 1976.

Ingersoll, Robert Green. *Greatest Speeches of Col. R. G. Ingersoll*. Chicago: Rhodes and McClure, 1985.

Works Cited

Jensen, Ellen. *Improvement Era Magazine*, Oct. 1929.

Kimball, Spencer W. *Tragedy or Destiny?* Salt Lake City: Deseret Book, 1977.

Klebingat, Jörg. "Defending the Faith." Ensign Magazine, Sep. 2017.

Lee, Harold B. Area conference, Munich, Germany, 1973.

Lewis, C. S. *Mere Christianity*. San Francisco: Harper-Collins, 1943.

——. *Weight of Glory*. San Francisco: Harper-Collins, 2015.

Lundahl, Craig R. "Angels in Near Death Experiences." Journal of Near-Death Studies, 11(1), Fall 1992, 53.

Maxwell, Neal A. *But for a Small Moment*. Salt Lake City: Deseret Book, 1986.

——. "Apply the Atoning Blood of Christ." General Conference, Oct. 1997.

——. "Endure It Well." General Conference, Apr. 1990.

——. "How Choice a Seer!" General Conference, Oct. 2010.

——. "Premortality, a Glorious Reality." General Conference, Oct. 1985.

——. *The Promise of Discipleship*. Salt Lake City: Deseret Book, 2001. Elder Maxwell wrote more than thirty books. This particular book includes a chapter about the spirit world, which he had particularly studied the last six years of his life as he suffered from leukemia. This book was completed just three years before the disease took his life.

——. "The Women of God." General Conference, Apr. 1978.

——. "Yet Thou Art There." General Conference, Oct. 1987.

"Vickie M. "Out of Body Experience." NDE, NDERF, www.nderf.org/nderfexplorer/nderf_.html, retrieved January 10, 2022.

McConkie, Bruce R. "The Dead Who Die in the Lord." General Conference, Oct. 1976.

Menet, Sarah LaNell. *There Is No Death*. Phillipsburg, MT: Mountain Top, 2002.

Moody, Raymond. *Life after Life*. Covington, GA: Mockingbird Books, 1975. In this early scientific study of NDEs, Moody explores experiences that are common to many who have experienced an NDE. He also expresses some of the weakness of science that inhibits it recognizing NDEs.

——. *The Light Beyond*. New York: Bantam Books, 1988. Moody has not personally experienced an NDE, but he has made a study of the experiences of others and has written several books. This one offers synopses of the work of several researchers. He feels that NDEs have two irrefutable proofs: 1) everyone he knows of who has experienced an NDE (including those researched by others) has returned happier and more dedicated to higher purposes than before, and 2) many who have experienced an NDE can give precise detail of the events in the hospital (even some that occurred in a different area in the hospital) while the person was "dead."

——. *Reflections on Life After Life*. Covington, GA: Mockingbird Books, 1978.

Neal, Mary C. *To Heaven and Back*. Colorado Springs, CO: WaterBrook Press, 2013.

Nelson, Lee. *Beyond the Veil*, vol. 1. Springville, UT: Cedar Fort, 1988.

Nelson, Wendy. "Sister Wendy Nelson's Remarks," Worldwide Youth Devotional, June 3, 2018.

Osis, Karlis and Haraldsson, Erlundur. *At the Hour of Death*. Norwalk, CN: Hastings House, 1997.

Pewresearch.com. "Christians remain world's largest religious group, but they are declining in Europe." April 5, 2017.

Rampton, Ryan. J. *You Were Born a Warrior: A Near Death Experience*. Independently published, 2018.

Ring, Kenneth, PhD. *Heading Toward Omega*. New York: Quill, 1984. Like Dr. Moody's books, this book is a scientific study of NDEs, garnered from 111 peoples' experiences. Ring focuses much of his book on how an NDE affects the rest of a person's life.

Ritchie, George G., Jr. *Ordered to Return*. Charlottesville, VA: Hampton Roads, 1998. The follow-up book to Return from Tomorrow, this book is a magnificent example of how an NDE can enhance one's life. Dr. Ritchie believes that his orientation to the spirit world was hosted by the Savior. Dr. Ritchie thereafter dedicated his life to advocating Christ and exhorting others to follow His example. As a follower of Christ, he has tried to especially serve the downtrodden.

——. *Return from Tomorrow*. Grand Rapids, MI: Baker Book House, 1978. This book essentially "opened the door" for lending credence to NDEs and it has been immensely popular. My copy, printed in 2004, was from the thirty-third printing. Ritchie's obvious character and multiple advanced degrees (including a doctorate in psychiatry) lend him great respect and credibility.

Rotstein, Gary. "Near Death, Seeing Dead People May Be Neither Rare nor Eerie." Standard Examiner Newspaper, Ogden, UT: July 10, 2018.

Works Cited

Scott, Richard G. "Jesus Christ Our Redeemer." General Conference, Apr. 1997.

Si, William. "Meeting a Loving Being of Light." NDERF, www.nderf.org/nderfexplorer/nderf_.html, retrieved January 10, 2002.

Smith, Joseph Fielding, *Doctrines of Salvation*, Deseret Book, 1905.

——. *Teachings of the Prophet Joseph Smith*, Deseret News Press, 1938.

Smith, Lucy M. *The Revised and Enhanced History of Joseph Smith by His Mother*. Salt Lake City: Bookcraft, 1996.

Smith, Joseph F. *Gospel Doctrine*, 1919, 16th printing.

Sobes, Victor Z. "Going Through a Tunnel." NDERF, www.nderf.org/nderfexplorer/nderf.html, retrieved January 10, 2022.

Springer, Rebecca Ruter. *My Dream of Heaven*. LaVerne, TN: White Crow Books, 2009.

Teachings of Presidents of the Church: Brigham Young, BYU Press, Priesthood/Relief Society manual, 1997.

Teachings of Presidents of the Church: Harold B. Lee, BYU Press, Priesthood/Relief Society manual, 2000.

Top, Brent L., and Wendy C. *Glimpses Beyond Death's Door*. American Fork, UT: Covenant Communications, 2012.

Yancey, Philip. *The Jesus I Never Knew*. Grand Rapids, MI: Zondervon Publishing, 1995.

Young, Brigham. *Discourses of Brigham Young*. Compiled by John A. Widstoe. Salt Lake City: Deseret Book, 1954.

Wesley M. White

INDEX

Adam & Eve, 49, 82
Alexander, Eben, 58, 63, 100, 112, 116, 118, 145, 149–150, 155, 162, 165, 182
Amulek, 174
Arrington, Leonard J., 175
Benson, Robert Hugh, 22–23, 26 48, 50–55, 58, 60–63, 68–71, 76–78, 79, 83, 86–88, 89, 92–93, 96, 101, 102–106, 109–110, 112, 116, 117, 120, 121–124, 125, 126, 129–130, 131, 132–135, 136, 141–142, 144, 150, 151, 152, 153–154, 157–159, 170, 172–173, 174–175
Benson, Ezra Taft, 5–6, 7, 81, 89
Book of Mormon, 99, 126, 127, 163, 174
Brother of Jared, 99–100
Burpo, Todd/Colton, 72, 73, 123, 128, 143–144, 145, 148, 155
Callister, Tad, 186–187, 191
Clark, J. Reuben, 27–28
Crowther, Duane S., 55, 63, 64, 131, 134, 136, 137
Doctrine and Covenants, 23, 32
Eadie, Betty, 30, 32, 34, 39, 47, 49, 55, 72, 73, 83, 89, 115, 117, 119–120, 124, 128, 130–131, 136
Edwin, 50–54, 92, 104, 109, 132, 133–134

Faust, James E., 28, 82, 89, 120, 128, 172, 175
Gong, Gerritt W., 188, 191
Hales, Robert D., 83, 89
Haraldsson, Erlendur, 170–172, 175
Heavenly Father, 3, 18, 26, 33, 163, 164, 184, 185, 188
Hill, Mary V., 32
Hinckley, Gordon B., 37, 38, 39
Holland, Elder Jeffrey R., 82–83, 89, 127–128
Holy Ghost, 9, 13–14, 46, 135–136, 163–165
Hunter, Howard W., 23, 28
Ingersoll, Robert Green, xviii
Jesus Christ/Savior, xx, xxi, 2, 10, 13, 18, 26, 27, 28, 33, 34, 35, 38, 39, 43, 44, 48, 49, 50, 59, 60, 61, 62, 66, 67, 72, 86, 88, 106, 112, 125, 126, 127, 130, 140, 145, 147, 154, 163, 164, 165, 175, 178, 179, 181, 182, 183–191
Kerr, Christopher, 167, 168
Kimball, Heber, 48
Kimball, Spencer W, 30, 32
Klebingat, Jörg, 2–3, 7
Lee, Harold B., 37–38, 39, 49, 76, 79
Lehi, 126–127

Lewis, C. S., 22, 28, 100–101, 113, 120, 128, 184, 186, 190, 191
Luke (Apostle), 29, 62, 187
Lundahl, Craig R., Ph.D, 85–86, 89
MacDonald, George, 28, 186
Matthias (Apostle), 86
Maxwell, Neal L., 1–7, 27–28, 33, 99, 102, 112, 119, 155, 187–188, 191
McConkie, Bruce R., 5, 7, 31–32
Menet, Sarah LaNell, 57, 61, 62, 64, 124, 128
Moody, Raymond, xx, 6, 36–37, 39, 112, 117, 129, 130, 134, 136, 148, 152, 155, 162, 165, 177–178, 182
Moses, 33, 99, 100, 111, 153, 181, 184
Neal, Mary C., 36, 39, 41, 43, 46, 131, 136, 151, 155, 161, 162–163, 165
Nelson, Lee, 30, 32, 63
Nephi, 181
Osis, Karlis, 170–172, 175
Pratt, Orson, 120–121, 151
Pratt, Parley P., 48, 62
Rachel's Stories, 9–14, 39, 78–79, 88, 94, 101–102, 135–136, 145, 163–165, 175,
Rampton, Ryan J., 38, 39
Ring, Kenneth, PhD, 75, 79, 145, 161, 165, 182
Ritchie, George G., xix, xx, 2, 6, 37, 39, 44, 46, 48, 55, 58, 59, 62, 63 64, 66, 72–73, 100, 110–112, 113, 162, 165, 178, 182, 191
Roger, 50–54, 123
Roncevich, Beth, 167–168

Rotstein, Gary, 167–169, 175
Ruth, 50 –54, 104, 109, 123
Samuel the Lamanite, 63
Satan/Lucifer, 23, 26, 27, 30, 33, 67
Scott, Richard G., 29, 32, 183, 188, 191
Si, William, 44–45, 46
Smith, Emma Hale, 139–140, 172
Smith, Joseph, 4, 31, 72, 75, 76, 81, 91, 100, 102, 123, 129, 135, 139–140, 141, 169, 172, 181
Smith, Joseph F., 39, 49, 82, 95, 141
Smith, Lucy Mack, 145
Smith, Mary Fielding, 141
Snow, Eliza R., 139, 144
Sobes, Victor Z., 43, 46
Springer, Rebecca Ruter, 91–92, 94, 106–108, 113, 125–126, 128
Swedenborg, Emmanuel, 48, 95, 100, 135, 140–141, 144, 152–153
Taylor, John, 31, 147, 148
Top, Brent L. and Wendy C., 48, 55, 63, 89, 95, 96, 97, 112, 128, 137, 145, 155, 161, 165
White, Kay, 14, 24, 84, 144
White, Russell, 17, 144
Yancey, Philip, 185, 190, 191
Young, Brigham, 37, 39, 48, 49, 55, 64, 66–68, 73, 147, 155, 169, 175

Wesley M. White

Wesley M. White

Made in the USA
Columbia, SC
06 January 2025